What people are saying about …

An Untroubled Heart

"I am happy to recommend this precious student and teacher of God's Word to you. Micca has lived out what she believes. You can learn much from this woman who has passed His tests with flying colors of faith because she knows her God and feeds on His Word."

Kay Arthur, Co-CEO of Precept Ministries International

"Micca writes with the heart of a wife and mother who has known bad times and good times. She speaks with honesty and humility."

Jan Silvious, author of *Big Girls Don't Whine*

"Through captivating personal stories and biblical truths, Micca reveals how to overcome the crippling peace-robbers of fear and worry. Penned from firsthand experiences, these heart-felt pages spill over with understanding, transparency, and wisdom."

Ginger Plowman, national speaker, author of *Heaven at Home*

"This book is a must read for everyone who treads the path of faith. Micca explores the doubts and fears that complicate our trust in God and then guides the reader into deep assurance of God's trustworthiness with her honesty, vulnerability, and a touch of humor."

Susanne Scheppmann, author of *Divine Prayers for Despairing Parents*

"*An Untroubled Heart* is a gift to anyone who has experienced pain, fear, and hopelessness. Micca ties together the lives of biblical and modern-day people to create a survival kit for the wounded heart."

Mary Southerland, author of *Hope in the Midst of Depression*

"Micca is a rare combination of Bible teacher, best friend, and girl-next-door. Her laid back Southern charm leaps off the pages as she takes you by the hand and leads you to a faith that is stronger than all your fears."

LeAnn Rice, executive director of Proverbs 31 Ministries

"Like living room conversations with a close friend, Micca shares her fears, vulnerabilities, and faith in a way that causes readers to learn as much about themselves as they do the storyteller."

Dave Clark, songwriter

"Micca is well acquainted with the One who overcomes the world, and in this book she highlights the essential truths that can help us experience an untroubled heart no matter what comes our way."

Cheri Keaggy, Dove Award winning recording artist

"I know the struggle of anxiety all too well and I can honestly say that this is one of the most authentic and relevant books I've read on the topic. Micca challenged me to look to the source of my fears and focus on knowing and trusting Jesus as the One True Remedy.

Lindsey Kane, Christian recording artist

"Micca offers hurting hearts a warm blanket of truth and reassurance in a very cold and uncertain world. She presents the Word of God in a way that speaks deep into my heart."

Glynnis Whitwer, author of *When Your Child Is Hurting*

"Micca's story will captivate you. Her humor will delight you. Her girlfriend style will have you eagerly turning the pages. And her biblical wisdom will have you highlighting pages like crazy."

Lysa TerKeurst, author, speaker, and president of Proverbs 31 Ministries

an
untroubled
heart

finding a faith that is stronger than all my fears

micca campbell

David C Cook®
transforming lives together

AN UNTROUBLED HEART
Published by David C Cook
4050 Lee Vance View
Colorado Springs, CO 80918 U.S.A.

David C Cook Distribution Canada
55 Woodslee Avenue, Paris, Ontario, Canada N3L 3E5

David C Cook U.K., Kingsway Communications
Eastbourne, East Sussex BN23 6NT, England

The graphic circle C logo is a registered trademark of David C Cook.

All Scripture quotations, unless otherwise noted, are taken from the *Holy Bible,
New International Version*®. *NIV*®. Copyright © 1973, 1978, 1984 by International
Bible Society. Used by permission of Zondervan. All rights reserved. Scripture
quotations marked NKJV are taken from the New King James Version. Copyright
© 1982 by Thomas Nelson, Inc. Used by permission. All rights reserved. Scripture
quotations marked MSG are taken from *THE MESSAGE*. Copyright © by Eugene H.
Peterson 1993, 1994, 1995, 1996, 2000, 2001, 2002. Used by permission of NavPress
Publishing Group. Verses marked TLB are taken from *The Living Bible,* © 1971,
Tyndale House Publishers, Wheaton, IL 60189. Used by permission.

LCCN 2008942921
ISBN 978-1-4347-6797-4
eISBN 978-0-7814-0713-7

© 2009 Micca Campbell
Published in association with William K. Jensen Literary Agency,
119 Bampton Court, Eugene, OR 97404.

The Team: Terry Behimer, Karen Lee-Thorp, Sarah
Schultz, Jaci Schneider, and Caitlyn York
Cover Design: Amy Kiechlin
Cover Photo: Getty Images, Digital Vision Collection, Kathrin Ziegler

Printed in the United States of America
First Edition 2009

5 6 7 8 9 10

021313

Contents

To my beloved pastor, James R. Moore, who is now at
home in the presence of the One he so faithfully served.

Your example taught me to love people, to trust God in the
good times and the bad, to laugh at life, to fear nothing,
to put family first, to respond with grace and dignity in
all situations, to be the first to apologize, and to lead by
serving. You were more than my pastor: You were my friend
and mentor whom I love dearly for loving me so greatly.

Acknowledgments

To my wonderful husband Pat—because of your constant love, support, and encouragement, I'm able to walk the path God has laid before me. I love you.

To my kids—Mitch, Peyton, and Parker—thank you for sacrificing your mom in various ways as I spent many long days dedicating my time to this book. I love that you gave in order for others to find truth. You three are my most precious earthly treasures.

To my mom and dad, who saw my God-given abilities long before I ever did—thank you for not only believing in me, but for giving me a heritage of faith to stand on. It's the one thing that has sustained me throughout my life.

To my in-laws, Nancy and Joe Campbell—thank you for being available and stepping in when I needed help with the kids. Your support is greatly appreciated.

To my prayer team—JoAnn Armour, Ann Barkley, and Sandy Martian. The thing we do for the kingdom is not our true work—prayer is. Thank you for your faithful prayer support. It was the avenue through which God directed and inspired this book.

To my agent, Bill Jensen—thank you for believing in my story. Your friendship and many years of experience paid off! I love working with you.

To Lysa Terkeurst, Renee Swope, Leann Rice, and the team of Proverbs 31 Ministries—I value each of your friendships. Thank you for believing in me, dreaming with me, praying for me, and cheering me on to victory! I couldn't have done it without you.

To my dear friend Bonita Lillie—thank you for being my second pair of eyes and for using your talent to put an extra shine on mine. Your encouragement and friendship mean the world to me.

To Karen—thank you for going beyond the duties of editor to provide me with wisdom and direction. I greatly appreciate and admire your editorial expertise and passion for the written word.

To Terry and all those at David C. Cook—thank you for taking this journey with me! It's been a blast!

To my Lord Jesus Christ, who has trusted me with His Word and allowed me to speak His life-changing truths into the hearts of others. May He alone be glorified.

Introduction

In writing this book, I was often asked, "Don't you have fears too?" The answer is yes. People naturally assume that since I'm writing on the subject of worry and anxiety, I have conquered all my own fears. I can honestly say that I have been liberated from most of my fears by placing my faith in God instead of in my circumstances. Still, some fears sneak up on me unaware. I find myself worrying about my children, my health, world events, and walking alone in the mall parking lot at night. Sound familiar?

Since you're reading this book, I imagine you struggle with anxiety too. You and I are not alone. Thousands of people live with fear and anxiety every day. Fear is a very real, personal, and powerful emotion. Throughout my life and ministry, I've met people who are concerned about a failing economy. Others are hesitant and suspicious of anyone different from themselves. Worried parents are cautious about letting their children out of sight for fear of abduction. Nearly everyone fears death. Whether it's our own death or the death of someone we love, the unknown factors of how and when it will happen frighten us the most. I think it was a country music singer who once said, "It's not that I'm afraid to die. I just don't want to be there when it happens." Those are my thoughts exactly!

We all have something that frightens us. Perhaps the thing that terrifies us most is losing control and realizing our helplessness. In the face of the unthinkable, the unbearable, or the unimaginable, fear uncovers

truth. We're not really in control of anything. Control is only an illusion. When the unthinkable happens, and we lose a loved one, we're
gripped not only by great pain, but also by great fears as our illusions of
control become shattered. I know, because it happened to me.

On the other hand, realizing our helplessness isn't as bad as
you might imagine. It's often the beginning of a new thing—a new
dependence on God who is sovereign over all. In simpler words, He's
large and in charge! Therefore there's nothing to fear when you and I
are certain that God is in control and on our side.

I heard a story about five-year-old Johnny who was in the kitchen
as his mother made supper. She asked him to go into the pantry and get
her a can of tomato soup, but he didn't want to go in alone. "It's dark in
there and I'm scared." She asked again, and he persisted. Finally she said,
"It's okay—Jesus will be in there with you." Johnny walked hesitantly to
the door and slowly opened it. He peeked inside, saw it was dark, and
started to leave when all at once an idea came, and he said: "Jesus, if
you're in there, would you hand me that can of tomato soup?"[1]

Like Johnny, we'd be less fearful if we knew for sure Jesus was there to
hand us our can of soup instead of having to get it alone. The truth is we
don't have to go it alone. Jesus has promised to never leave us nor forsake
us. By putting my trust in this promise, my life has been transformed. I've
developed a faith stronger than all my fear. I'm certain you can too.

Whatever you and I face throughout the year, we need not worry.
God has broken the spirit of fear and given us the assurance that
nothing can snatch us from His hand. As God's children, we can go
to Him without hesitation and cry out, "Abba, Father," which means
"Daddy," confident that He will hear and answer our cries—and, if
need be, hand us a can of soup.

Chapter One
When the Unthinkable Happens

Sometimes Porter would meet me in my dreams. One of those imag-
inings is forever etched in my mind. In the dream, I found myself
exploring stored treasures in my grandmother's garage, just like I did
when I was a girl. The sky was a brilliant blue and the grass was greener
than ever before. Granny's blooming spring flowers gave a fresh fra-
grance to the staleness of the garage. As I strolled through the garage,
admiring its contents, my thoughts were interrupted by the sound
of someone dribbling a basketball. I looked up, and there he was.
"Porter," I whispered to myself. He was so beautiful that he glowed.
I had forgotten what a magnificent creature he was. The last time I
had seen him, he had been blackened and disfigured by the fire. Now
his perfect, muscular body stood before me, whole again, just like I
remembered before the accident.

Slowly, he bounced the ball as he walked down the sidewalk
toward me. Bounce. Bounce. Bounce. I couldn't take my eyes off of
him for fear that if I blinked, he might disappear. Porter didn't say a
word. He gently took me by the hand and led me underneath a huge
oak tree, where he sat down on the basketball. I would have followed

him anywhere at that point. In his soft, soothing voice that I'd waited so long to hear again, he consoled me.

"I want you to know that I'm okay, and you're going to be okay too," he said. I longed for that moment to last forever, but I awoke.

For some time after that, bedtime became a ritual. I laid my head down on my pillow, closed my eyes, and whispered with hope, "See you in my dreams, Porter." At night, I found comfort in knowing that he just might meet me there.

Fairy Tale Romance

Fairy tales are what dreams are made of. From the time we begin to explore our world as toddlers, we dream. A little boy dreams of fighting battles, rescuing damsels, and becoming the king of his castle. A young girl dreams about finding her knight in shining armor, mothering a houseful of babies, and living happily ever after. For most, dreams do come true. We fall in love, conquer our battles, and nurture a family along the way. For others, dreams unexpectedly turn into nightmares. Such was the case with me.

I was nineteen when I met Porter. He was such a looker that my friends had only one word to describe him—"Mercy!" He worked loading boxes of frozen foods onto eighteen-wheelers, so his body was chiseled and fit. He had a cute little dimple in the middle of his chin and a picture-perfect smile. His eyes were like deep pools of rich chocolate framed by brown, wavy hair that nestled on his collar. Most important was his way of seeing the best in me and others, always putting the needs of his family, friends, and coworkers before himself. This sincere and kind attribute attracted many and gained their respect. Porter was the perfect package, both inside and out.

At first glance, "Mercy!" was the best word to describe him, but after one date, I was deeply in love. I knew this person, who didn't even kiss on the first date, was the one for me. Once I made up my mind that he was my man, I just had to make up *his* mind that *I* was the right choice for him—and then we got married. It felt as if the whole world had been created just for us. Nothing could penetrate our circle of love. I had found my Prince Charming, and I planned to live happily ever after.

We were poor as church mice, so there wasn't much money for entertainment. We spent our spare time snuggled together on the couch in our small duplex, eating potato chips and fantasizing about the future. Sometimes we talked into the wee hours of the morning sharing secrets like best friends and naming our unborn children. On Saturdays we took long drives on Porter's motorcycle. I was happy with my arms wrapped securely around his waist, my hair blowing in the wind. It didn't matter that we had nowhere in particular to go. It only mattered that we were together.

After a year and a half of marriage, God blessed us with a beautiful baby boy. My life was a fairy tale. First I became a wife, and now I was a mother. I was living my childhood dream just as I had planned—until the night Porter didn't come home.

Shattered Dreams

Dinner was getting cold. I was pacing the floor with the baby on my hip, wondering where he could be, when my father knocked at the door. Immediately, I could tell something was wrong. "What is it, Dad?" I asked cautiously.

"Porter has been in an accident," he said.

I didn't stop to consider that Porter could be seriously hurt. That was simply out of the question. Instead, I quickly phoned a friend to keep the baby and concentrated on packing the diaper bag with everything our son might need. I only prepared a few bottles, since I assumed Porter would be discharged when I arrived, and we would all be home together again later that evening.

Once our son was settled at the babysitter's house and Dad and I were on were on way to the hospital, there was nothing else to occupy my mind. I couldn't help but think about the accident. "How bad is it?" I asked Dad, searching for clues in his face.

"I really don't know. I think … well … what I mean is I'm not clear about what happened. The neighbors said there was … uh … some sort of explosion. We'll know more when we get there." He stumbled over every word.

It seemed like we had been driving for a long time without making progress. With every mile my heart grew more anxious. I imagined every bad thing I could think of and then prayed it wasn't so. I couldn't stop wondering what went wrong that caused his accident.

Earlier that morning, Porter had gone to my brother-in-law's house to help him waterproof his basement. The day before, my brother-in-law had dug a seven-foot ditch around the foundation of the house with a backhoe so that Porter could apply the water-proofing substance to the outside wall. Realizing the substance was highly flammable, Porter felt confident that working outdoors would allow the fumes to escape and prevent any danger. Unfortunately, as they worked, the fumes mounted in the ditch. When they had only five feet left to finish, the outside heating and air conditioning unit clicked on to cool the inside of the house. The fumes ignited, and the ditch exploded. The blast of fire left Porter and our brother-in-law badly burned over the majority of their bodies.

They were lucky, though. A fire truck was only three houses away. Neighborhood friends shared with us that firemen had been called to a nearby home to save an elderly man who choked on his dinner. By the time the firemen arrived, the food had dislodged and all was well. As the two firemen were returning to their truck, they spotted my sister's house in flames only a short distance away. Another neighbor added details to the conversation about what she saw. Apparently our husbands were in shock. Badly burned, they stripped off the rest of their clothes and began spraying themselves with the garden hose. Immediately, the firemen placed our husbands on gurneys, loaded them into the truck, and rushed them to Vanderbilt Burn Center.

When my dad and I arrived at the burn center, my mom and sister were already there. The nurse escorted all of us to a small room where the doctor tried to prepare us for what we were about to see. His explanation was quick and to the point. My brother-in-law had been burned over 40 percent of his body, but they expected full recovery. My husband, on the other hand, had been burned over 80 percent of his body, both inside and out. They gave him a fifty-fifty chance of survival.

Until Death Do Us Part

It was a long walk with the doctor as he led my sister and me to see our husbands. I felt numb inside. The activity in the hospital appeared to move in slow motion while the echo of our footsteps rang in my ears. I think I held my breath all the way. When we got to their room, I froze just inside the door. I couldn't tell who was who. Their skin was completely black. Their heads were twice the normal size, and Porter's forearms were wrapped in towels because most of his flesh had been burned. They were unrecognizable. Suddenly, the room grew dim, and my body went limp. Someone from behind caught me and held me up. I could hear my sister crying beside me, but I couldn't turn to her. I couldn't take my eyes off of the two horrid bodies in front of us. "Please, God. Don't let it be them," I prayed to myself. At that same moment, my brother-in-law spoke. "Hey, at least we're alive," he joked. We managed to walk over to them. Curious, I reached over to lift the towel from Porter's arm and take a peek, but the doctor immediately stopped me. "Those are to prevent infection," the physician explained as he tucked the cloth tightly back around Porter's arms. "We need to keep them covered. There's not much skin left. His hands and arms got the worst of it," he continued.

Stunned, I stepped back. "Hey, it's going to be all right," Porter said, trying to reassure me. He was right. They were alive.

"Surely, it can only get better from here, right, God?" I prayed silently. It was then that I felt strength come over me, carrying me on from that moment.

Over the next eight days, the waiting room was crowded with people. They were mostly quiet, not knowing what to say. Their presence spoke volumes to me. It spoke comfort, compassion, and love, especially on the day of Porter's surgery.

To prevent blood poisoning, the doctor was going to perform a procedure called skin grafting. After Porter went into surgery, the wait was long. It was so long that my mother became suspicious, wondering about the reason for the elapsed time. She encouraged us to eat the sandwiches our church family had brought. It was the last time that I remember eating for a long while.

Later, the doctor, still in his surgical clothes, walked slowly into the waiting room with his head hung low and his shoulders slouched. No one spoke a word. He slowly bent down in front of my chair and began confirming my worst fears. "In the middle of surgery, Porter went into cardiac arrest," he explained as gently as he could. "His burned body was unable to withstand the trauma of surgery, and it shut down." The waiting room was hushed and still. The doctor continued. "The good news is Porter could wake up within the next twenty-four hours."

I could feel my chest tighten. It was hard to breathe, as if the doctor were choking me with his every word. Before he could speak again, I stood up and took off running. I ran until I found myself on the roof of one of the hospital buildings. I suppose I had to get as close to God as possible. Who else could help me now?

While people shuffled along the sidewalk below, I wailed in deep sorrow as I begged God to save Porter. Pacing back and forth, I struggled with the thought that it might be better for Porter to be in the presence of the Lord than to live. "I should let him go," I thought. "At least in heaven, he will be fully restored and won't have any more pain. If he lives, I know for sure he won't keep his arms," I reasoned to myself. But—"No!" Call it selfish. I didn't care. I was desperate. It didn't matter to me that Porter would never be able to hold me again or throw a ball with his son. I just wanted Porter to live. But God had other plans.

As the clock ticked down, there was no response. The doctor tested for brain waves and found none. Soon, Porter's organs began to shut down too. As I sat there beside him, I knew he had already left me. Days before his surgery, as he lay in excruciating pain that not even high doses of morphine could ease, Porter tried to tell me his time was short. He knew that he was going away, but I refused to listen. Each day, my sweet husband attempted to comfort and prepare me, saying, "I don't want to leave you and our son, but I know my time has come." He was right. I knew that now, but I couldn't let go of him. I just couldn't. As I struggled with my thoughts, a nurse entered the room and began to fiddle with his life-support machine.

"Can I ask you something?" I inquired of her.

"Sure, honey, what is it?" the nurse replied.

"If you were to turn off my husband's machine, he wouldn't breathe on his own ever again—would he?" I questioned.

The nursed paused for a moment, and then, turning to me, she confirmed softly, "No, honey, he wouldn't." Once again, I felt a strength that enabled me to do what I couldn't do alone.

I got up from my chair beside my husband's bed and walked into the crowded waiting room. "He's gone," I announced. My own words passed my consciousness and went straight to my heart, where they exploded in agony. Soft sniffling sounds began to move throughout the waiting room. Without saying a word or showing emotion, Porter's mother got up and walked slowly into her son's room. I followed her. Stopping just outside his door, I watched. She lay across her son's body, burst into tears, and gently began to caress his feet. They were the only part of Porter's body untouched by the fire. I turned and left them alone. Sometime thereafter, his life-giving machine was turned off by the doctor, and Porter passed from this life to the next.

Rescued from Despair

When the funeral was over, and the people were gone, I found myself alone, a new mother and a widow at the age of twenty-one. How would I get through this crisis? My dream had become a living nightmare from which I couldn't escape. Life was lonely without him. I felt deserted by my God, the God I had loved and served since I was a little girl. Why would He betray me? Why didn't Porter fight to live? It wasn't fair! This was not what I had planned.

One desperate night, I hit bottom. Grief-stricken, suicidal thoughts plagued my mind. Pacing the floor of my duplex, I found myself torn between living for my son and dying for my husband. Abruptly, my grief turned to anger until I did what any woman whose family had been destroyed would do. In my mind's eye, I burst through the door to the throne room of grace, shook my fist in the face of God, and boldly questioned, "WHY—why did You do this to me? You could have saved him! You're God! Why did You give me that baby and take his father? Oh, God, I need to know why!"

Just as a mother runs to her screaming child who is in pain, God the Father ran to me, His child. I didn't see Him with my eyes or touch Him with my hands, but I felt His presence consume me as if God poured Himself over my entire body. I couldn't cry another tear. God's presence was so calming and comforting that I knew for the first time beyond a shadow of doubt that I was going to be okay. I didn't know how, but I knew God was fully aware and involved in my circumstances. I could no longer deny it. As I sat in the presence of my heavenly Father, I was compelled to read Psalm 139. It was as if God was speaking directly to my heart.

> Where can I go from your Spirit?
> Where can I flee from your presence?
> If I go up to the heavens, you are there;
> if I make my bed in the depths, you are there.
> If I rise on the wings of the dawn,
> if I settle on the far side of the sea,
> even there your hand will guide me,
> your right hand will hold me fast. (Ps. 139:7–10)

Even in the pit of death, God had come to say, "You are not alone. I am here."

You Are Not Alone

It's funny. The newspapers called me a survivor. On most days, I didn't feel like a survivor, but I had survived. I had lived through my worst fear. But that didn't mean I would never fear losing another loved one. I do. Like Porter, his dad died young, so I fear that death at a young age is my son's destiny too. That's not all. Every time someone fails to call me when they are running late, I worry that the worst has happened. Is it right for me to be concerned? Are my fears legitimate? Probably so, but the good news is I don't have to live afraid, and neither do you.

Our present fears are fueled by our past experiences. Nevertheless, God doesn't want us to go through the rest of our lives justifying our fears. Nor does He want us to live behind some protective wall that shields us from what might happen. God wants to teach us that it's safe to trust Him. Even if we don't have all the answers, our past will never make sense until we invite God into our present. Then we will see He has been there all along.

My first step in learning to trust God again came when I chose to believe that I am never ever alone. God is always near me. Looking back, I realize the strength I felt in the midst of my suffering was God's presence carrying me through the valley of death safely to the other side. Time and again when I felt lost and alone, God met me in my pain and carried me to new levels of grace. With each encounter, my future grew brighter, and I was able to pick up the pieces of my shattered dream and with God's help rebuild my life.

The Lord is, indeed, attentive to our whereabouts and the circumstances we face on earth. He also knows how many days each of us will dwell here. This was an important truth for me concerning Porter's death.

> Your eyes saw my unformed body.
> All the days ordained for me
> were written in your book
> before one of them came to be. (Ps. 139:16)

God didn't take my husband from me. Porter's death wasn't a personal attack or payment for some sin I had committed. Nor had my heavenly Father left me to spin helplessly out of control. No—God, in His sovereignty, simply knew the number of Porter's years. I feel privileged to have been a part of his days and comforted in knowing that I'm not alone for the rest of mine.

It's easy to see God's hand at work in the lives of those who live between the pages of His Word. Yet through the course of our lives, especially during fearful times, God can seem so far away that we question, "Where are You, Lord?" No matter what our emotions or circumstances may say, the truth is there is nowhere we can go to escape God's presence. Though it might not feel like it or look like it, God is always near.

You may never have experienced God's presence in the powerful, comforting way that I did when my husband died, but that doesn't mean He is not with you. You and I are His masterpieces, "fearfully and wonderfully made" (Ps. 139:14) by the hands of a loving and faithful God. He is the God of all things great and small. He is the one who tells the sun when to rise and when to set. He is the God who causes the ocean waves to obey their boundaries. This is the God that gave life to you and me. Why would He do that and then leave us alone? He wouldn't. Just as a loving mother would never leave her child, God the Father will never leave us. He can't be torn away, led away, coaxed away, seduced away, or dragged away.

You and I come to know and experience this truth by faith. It is my prayer that as we journey together though the pages of this book, all of your fears will be replaced with unshakable faith in the One who is faithful and trustworthy in all things. As His child, may you truly learn to live carefree in the care of your heavenly Father.

Bible Study: Know It—Stow It—Show It

Loss is inevitable. We lose things every day. Some things are so small that we hardly notice, while others are so big they hurt—a lot. In any situation, God's presence is certain.

1. Recall a time when you felt afraid and alone. When was it?

2. Read Psalm 46:1. In times of trouble, what kind of help does God offer?

3. How does knowing that God is your ever-present help comfort you and calm your fears? (Or if it doesn't comfort you, talk about why.)

It calms my uncertainties to know that God's help is at hand immediately. It isn't a future help, nor is it available only when I'm worthy of God's help. No, it's a present help. God's help is available the moment we humble ourselves and cry out to Him.

4. Write James 1:2–4 here:

5. How do you view trials in your life? Are you fearful? Joyful? Angry? Do you see them as disastrous? Explain.

I have to be honest. It really annoys me that James says I should be joyful instead of fearful in hard times. I'd love to ask James, "Where's the joy when the divorce papers are served? Where's the joy when the doctor's diagnosis is bleak? What about when my teenager is living in rebellion? James, where's the joy when someone you love has died?" But over the years, I have learned that joy can be found in the midst of heartache and fearful times.

6. a. According to James 1:3, what are our trials producing in
      our lives? Explain in your own words.

   b. Where do you see that process at work in your life, if at all?

7. List the things found in verse 4 that develop from endurance
   or perseverance.

I desire to be perfect and complete, lacking in nothing. I just
don't want to have to go through a trial to get there. However, these
are the ways of God. When you and I can look to the end result of
what our testing is accomplishing, then we can find joy in the midst
of it. Ultimately, when adversity has its way, we mature. We change
from victim to victor! That, my friend, is a huge gain.

8. What Christlike qualities are you gaining or have you gained
   through the losses in your life?

9. Write a prayer thanking God for the good work He is doing
   in you and for helping you to conquer your fears in the process. Thank Him for being an ever-present help.

Chapter Two
The Fear Factor

Worry, fear, and anxiety were never meant to be a part of our vocabulary, and yet most of us worry more than we'd care to admit. What are you afraid of? Are you scared of waking up to an intruder in the middle of the night? Perhaps it's flying on an airplane. Maybe it's the fear of sending your child off to college. Does it frighten you when the phone rings and no one is there on the other end? Perhaps your greatest fear is not being able to provide for your family. Most of us can find something that haunts us.

Panic best describes the emotion I felt when the nurse rolled Jimmy out into the living room. Both of his legs had been amputated, and most of his fingers, too. Jimmy was the father of my son's friend from school. Beset with diabetes, he was at the end of his life. Hospice had been called in, but Jimmy refused to let go and cross over into eternity. Concerned about whether Jimmy knew the Lord or not, I had phoned his wife, Juanita, and asked if I could visit him. It was only a matter of time before he would come face-to-face with His Creator, and I wanted to be sure that Jimmy would meet Him as Savior and not as Judge.

Jimmy's deteriorating condition took me by surprise. When I saw him I was stunned, even terrified. I whispered to the Lord under my breath, "Oh, God, how can I minister to this man when I don't know what he's been through?" Even though I was scared stiff, somehow I knew God would show up to do what I couldn't do, and that's exactly what He did. As Jimmy and I talked, it was apparent that he knew the Father, but I sensed there was more. We weren't far into our conversation when I discovered the real trouble with Jimmy—he was afraid to die. I told Jimmy all the Bible stories about God sending angels to people in need, people just like him. Those angels had a special message: "Fear not, for God is with you!" As I shared with Jimmy, peace washed over his face as he received the message for himself.

It was at Jimmy's funeral that his wife shared his last moments with me. Jimmy would often wake from his sleep wide-eyed and call out, "I'm afraid!" Juanita would pat him gently and remind him of God's promise: "Don't be afraid, Jimmy. God is with you." Then he would sleep again. The last time Jimmy opened his eyes, he just stared at the ceiling. His wife asked, "Jimmy, are you afraid?" Jimmy whispered, "No, I'm not afraid. I'm just looking at the angels." With that, Jimmy stepped from this world into the next.

I find it interesting that while Jimmy's outcome didn't change, the way he experienced death did change because he trusted in the promise of God. I experienced this same truth in my life. Even though I pleaded with God to save Porter from death, it wasn't God's plan. Yet I chose to trust God's purpose. In spite of my fear, I chose to believe what I couldn't understand. Doing so changed the way I journeyed through the valley of death. I had a companion named Jesus.

Jimmy's story reminds me that when I'm afraid, I need not fret because the same promise God made to Jimmy, He makes to you and me: "Fear not, child, for I am with you." In fact, did you know that the phrase "fear not" is stated in the Bible 366 times? That's one "fear not" for every day of the year, with one extra left over for those really hard days. Why does God faithfully remind us over and over to "fear not"? He does so because we are not created to live in fear— "For God did not give us a spirit of timidity, but a spirit of power, of love and of self-discipline" (2 Tim. 1:7). You and I were created to live by faith, and in God, we have all the power we need for a faith that is stronger than all our fears.

It's a Problem of Faith

The truth is, most of what we worry about never comes to pass, but we insist on tormenting ourselves anyway. Worrying about what may or may not happen can nearly drive us crazy. It can keep us up at night and shut us down during the day. Let's face it—a lot can go wrong in life, but God doesn't want us to become worrywarts.

As you move through this book, you'll discover that for most people, fear is a faith problem rather than a psychological problem. It's a challenge of faith in a world where families are in conflict, jobs are insecure, morals are collapsing, and war and terrorism are daily realities. You'll discover how to balance pressure and stress without giving way to anxiety, and you'll recognize the promised presence of God guiding your daily life. You'll see how confidence in a faithful God unlocks the gateway to overcoming the fears of betrayal, loneliness, rejection, and the unknown.

It takes faith to battle fear and put to death our anxieties as we learn to live with assurance in a God we can bank on. Without faith, fear robs us of our peace, our abilities, our hopes, and our dreams.

Fearless Living

Let me ask you, how many times have you wanted to do something, plan something, build something, or even dream about something, but you were too afraid? You know deep within that your torment isn't right. You know you're missing out on life and opportunities, but you're too scared to do anything about it. My daughter has struggled with fear her entire life. We first noticed it when she was a baby. She would hold her breath when we carried her down a flight of stairs. Then, at the age of five, she passed out while riding the Ferris wheel at the state fair. Her fears sometimes hinder her from participating in life—from being an active contributor to society. Over the years, my heart has broken for her as I've watched her hold back from doing things she really wanted to do. Playing it safe only left her depressed. She lived most days looking at the world from behind a wall of safety glass, longing to be free. Freedom came when Peyton decided that she didn't want to live with regrets any longer. She pushed through her fear by exercising her faith in God. In doing so, her life is now marked by joy, peace, adventure, and courage.

Walking on Water

I wonder about the eleven disciples who stayed in the boat instead of stepping out onto the water like Peter. Did they live with regret? I don't know. But they did miss an amazing opportunity to walk on water with Christ! Sadly, most people stay in the safety of the boat their entire lives and wonder why life seems so empty, miserable, and dull. Those who live with anxiety are living below the mark of what they were created to be. Worry and its accompanying emotions are not and never were part of God's plan for His children.

Unfortunately, most people go through life missing opportunities because they're afraid to really live the way God intended. Fear becomes a stumbling block that not only trips us up but leaves us with regrets. Relying on our faith allows us to live fearlessly. Like Peter, we are then able to step out of the boat into a world of possibilities.

By God's Grace

I've learned that trusting God with one fear doesn't give me automatic faith for the next one. I still have my share of doubts. Writing this book is one of them. I realize it's a God-sized assignment that requires God-sized grace and power. Like Peter, instead of keeping my eyes on Christ, I usually attempt to walk on water in my own strength. I get dunked every time. Then I get discouraged, and I say things to myself like, "I knew I couldn't do this" or "I'm not good enough to take on such a task." In a way, I'm right. The truth is, I can't accomplish a God-sized project on my own, and God never intended me to do so. At the same time, He doesn't want me to anxiously fret over it. He doesn't want me to become discouraged and give up. No, He wants me to trust Him and allow His power to work through me to accomplish all He's called me to do. That's why I love to quote Paul's words in 1 Corinthians 15:10: "But by the grace of God I am what I am, and his grace to me was not without effect. No, I worked harder than all of them—yet not I, but the grace of God that was with me." It's only by God's grace that I can do anything! Although it's my responsibility to work hard and finish well the task God puts before me, I still need His grace and power to do so.

You and I came into this world poor, with nothing. God endowed us with gifts, abilities, personalities, creativity, and intelligence. Without these gifts, we are nothing and can do nothing. At the same time, with God anything is possible.

I get confused at times and think I'm supposed to accomplish the task alone, but then it becomes about me. The truth is, my biggest obligation is to maintain my relationship with God. When I lean on Him, my anxieties give way to peace.

It would be easy to give in to my fear and allow Satan to stop me. I could throw my manuscript up in the air and eat some gooey chocolate something. But I wouldn't feel better. I'd feel defeated. God didn't intend for you and me to live defeated. We were created to live by faith, not fear. We were made for greener pastures, where God's mercy and goodness dwell with us, provide for us, shelter us, and enable us to do whatever God is calling us to do—be a parent, a schoolteacher, a musician, a writer, or maybe even someone who walks on water.

When Peter threw one leg over the side of the boat, nobody believed he could walk on water. And while that thought was still fresh in the minds of his friends, Peter was already doing it. He was walking on water! Is there someone in your life planting doubt in your heart and mind over something you're already doing? If so, don't listen. Don't look back. Keep your eyes on Jesus and keep walking on water.

The Introduction of Fear

Have you ever wondered where our struggle between faith and fear began? Where the Devil got his foothold of fear in our lives? I have. According to Bible teacher Malcolm Smith, fear was introduced to the human race by a satanic lie.[1]

The garden is the first place where the serpent deceived Eve by twisting God's word. The Lord told Adam and Eve they could eat of any tree in the garden except the Tree of Knowledge. If they ate from that tree, they would surely die.

> Now the serpent was more crafty than any of the wild animals the LORD God had made. He said to the woman, "Did God really say, 'You must not eat from any tree in the garden'?" (Gen. 3:1)

Not only did Eve eat the forbidden fruit, but she also said to Adam, "Here, dummy, eat this." And he did. "Therefore, just as sin entered the world through one man, and death through sin, and in this way death came to all men, because all sinned" (Rom. 5:12).

It happened something like this:

After a grand tour of the garden, God presented the Tree of Knowledge to Adam and Eve. And the first thing He said was, "Don't."

"Don't what?" asked Adam.

"Don't eat the forbidden fruit," God said.

"Forbidden fruit? We have forbidden fruit? Hey, Eve, we have forbidden fruit!" cried Adam.

"No way!"

"Yes, way!"

"DO NOT EAT the fruit," God told them.

"Why?" Adam whined.

"Because I am your Father, and I said so!" God replied. (So that's where that came from.)

A few minutes later, God saw His children having an apple break, and boy, was He ticked. "Didn't I tell you not to eat the fruit?" God asked.

"Uh-huh," Adam replied.

"Then why did you?" the Father asked.

"I don't know," said Eve.

"She started it," shouted Adam.

"Did not!"

"Did too!"

Having had it with the two of them, God's punishment was that Adam and Eve should have children of their own.[2]

After Adam and Eve sinned against God, they were afraid and hid. "The LORD God called to the man, 'Where are you?' He answered, 'I heard you in the garden, and I was afraid because I was naked; so I hid'" (Gen. 3:9–10). As soon as Adam disobeyed God, their relationship changed. Adam was not only afraid, but he doubted God's authority, friendship, and provision. Satan's lie convinced Adam that he didn't need God. In fact, Adam was persuaded that he could be his own god, self-sufficient in every way.

The same is true for you and me. Most of the time, you and I live independent of God's presence. We act as if everything depends on us. We wouldn't dare admit that we are in over our heads. We want to appear in control. But God never meant for you and me to be strong in and of ourselves. We were meant to show His strength in our weakness as He provides for our needs. We were created to live like little children, dependent on the care our heavenly Father. However,

if we insist on living life our way, in our own strength, we will experience the same result as Adam and Eve. We will live in fear. This is
right where Ole Smutty Face (as my family refers to Satan) wants us.
If we're afraid to get out of the boat, we never will. If the Enemy can
keep us contained, we won't be able make a difference in the life of
another. Ole Smutty Face knows what we are capable of with Christ.
To prevent us from walking on water, he poisons us with fear.

False Advertisement

My youngest son loves chocolate milk. One day as I stirred syrup
into a tall glass of milk, I noticed that the label on the bottle read
"Genuine Artificial Flavor." I was shocked! What appeared to be real,
look real, and taste real was actually artificial! As I stood there in disbelief, I felt cheated and deceived. This was false advertisement.

In the same way, the Father of Lies specializes in false advertisement. He's good at making our fears—based on lies—look real when
they are not. In fact, Satan's greatest tool for causing us to doubt
God's care for our lives is the fear that God will not follow through
with His promises. The Enemy works hard to convince us that God
is too busy to do anything about our concerns. If anything is going
to be done about our situation, we'll have to do it ourselves. Like the
boogeyman, Satan's spooks are all smoke and mirrors. We can easily
expose his trickery by determining if there is really something to fear
or if our concerns are simply …

   False
   Evidence
   Appearing
   Real

This acrostic for fear is the kind of shock wave Satan uses to stun us. While the sting of fright feels real, in truth it's merely the trickery of Satan that gets our heart pounding. It's important for you and me to determine if our fears are real or simply Satan's hocus-pocus. If it's a real concern, I heed its warning. On the other hand, if my worry is false evidence that just appears real, then I know the Enemy is involved.

Good Fear, Bad Fear

On the upside, not all fear is bad. Some fear is healthy. Healthy fear is a natural feeling of alarm caused by imminent danger, pain, the unexpected, or disaster. This is a good type of fear. It alerts us to real danger much like flashing emergency lights warn us of hazardous situations. Good fear cautions us not to step out into oncoming traffic or disobey our boss for fear of the consequences. This is the exact definition of godly fear. We respectfully obey the ways of God and the laws of our society due to fear of the consequences.

However, when we have an abundance of bad fear that steals our peace and rest, we are lacking in the fear of God. Perhaps it's because we don't truly understand godly fear. To fear God is to reverence Him; it's to stand in awe of Him. Do you think we've lost the fear of God today? Do we reverence Him as we should? Do we stand in awe of His greatness and majesty? I think not. Perhaps we lack godly fear in our world today because most view God as a judge—someone who will punish sin. He is a judge, but God is also willing to forgive our sin if we will only ask. When we experience a healthy fear of God, we come to understand His love for us. Only then do we see that His "perfect love drives out fear" (1 John 4:18).

We don't live in terror of people who love us. We respect them. Likewise, a person who loves the Lord will live with a good measure of reverential fear. Their fear of the consequences of their actions motivates them to walk in obedience, yielding their will to God's will—but not out of duty. Their desire is to please the Lord who loves them.

Often, we are most afraid of surrendering to God's will. We fear that if we bend our will to conform to God's desires, He might send us to some remote wilderness as a missionary. One of the hardest things to do is to give up control and trust someone other than ourselves. Again, we misunderstand the benefit of a surrendered life. It's not about giving up; it's about gaining the power and presence of God living His life through us.

While godly fear is beneficial, the wrong type of fear that doubts God's loving care is unhealthy. This is Satan's job. He often takes what is meant for good and twists it into something damaging. Therefore, you and I must always be on guard.

Be Careful Where You Step

I learned to be on guard from the Enemy one spring day when my husband and I went for a walk on the nature trail in a park. We were on our last lap when suddenly I noticed a long black snake lying like a stick on my side of the trail. I stopped dead in my tracks and let out a piercing scream. The snake kept his position while my husband turned and ran the other way. I knew then that I was on my own!

My husband remembers the event differently. He recalls protecting me from the snake by fearlessly attacking it with his bare hands, whirling it around, and slinging it back into the woods. Supposedly, I rushed to him with rewards of hugs and kisses while exclaiming, "Oh, my hero, you saved me from that evil snake!" What puzzles me is how two people experiencing the same incident can walk away with two different stories! In thinking through that event, I wonder how many times on our walk we passed that snake, completely unaware of his presence. Now when we walk, I'm on guard, looking for the snake behind every bush and tree.

As you and I walk through the Christian life, we need to be aware of another snake. He is described as "that serpent of old, called the Devil and Satan, who deceives the whole world" (Rev. 12:9 NKJV). During our journey through life, we will encounter the Enemy on our path from time to time. He can show up in different forms such as trials, fears, broken relationships, discouragement, failures, and temptations. Yet our Lord has provided a way for us to stand guard against the Devil's tactics. "Submit yourselves, then, to God. Resist the devil, and he will flee from you" (James 4:7).

You and I can guard against the Devil by remembering that Christ conquered him on the cross. Satan no longer holds us in bondage to fear. When apprehensions come, our faith falters. We stand guard against the Devil by remembering God's words are true: "Never will I leave you; never will I forsake you" (Heb. 13:5). Resisting the Enemy is another way to guard ourselves. While he still has the power to tempt us, we can experience victory. As we submit to God and believe His truth instead of doubting it, the Devil will flee.

Finally, we must daily "put on the full armor of God so that you can take your stand against the devil's schemes" (Eph. 6:11). When we dress ourselves each day in God's armor, it acts as a hedge of protection that keeps the Enemy from showing up on our path and burdening us with hardships.

Satan has always been in the business of false advertisement and deception. False illusions are simply the Enemy's attempt to steal our peace. And fear becomes an obsession with ourselves as we attempt to be our own god. Yet, in the garden, God walked with Adam and Eve in the cool of the day. They lived in the Lord's presence without any cares. God was their provision for all things. Could it be this is still God's desire—for you and me to live fully in His care? You bet it is! Yet fear causes us to forfeit the benefits of His presence, His power, and His provision. For you and me to live as carefree children in the care of God, we must return to living daily in His presence. That's what this book is about. Since the beginning of time, we've stepped out of the care of God. The result has been fear. God has faithfully been calling us back to live in His love and care ever since. Faith in God's provision is our anchor that secures a life free from fear.

You may be skeptical right now, but at some point as you read this book, you're going to realize that you were created for faith, not fear. That's when things will begin to change for you. You'll learn how to rely on God's care while giving Him your cares, you'll be able to identify His goodness and mercy in your life, and you'll overcome your fears of loneliness and insecurity. What's more, you'll fall in love with God and learn to reverence Him as you practice His presence in prayer. Before you know it, you'll be able to say along with Paul, "I can do all things through Christ who strengthens me. I can even walk on water."

Bible Study: Know It—Stow It—Show It

1. Do you find it easier to believe Satan's lies or God's truths?
   Explain why.

2. a. What fears do you have today?

   b. How can you determine if those fears are simply False
      Evidence Appearing Real or things you ought to be con-
      cerned about?

3. What do the following verses say about Satan?
   Genesis 3:1–5

   John 8:44

   2 Corinthians 4:4

   1 Peter 5:8

   Revelation 12:9

4. In comparison, look up these verses and record what they say
   about Jesus:

Isaiah 9:6

John 8:12

John 10:11

John 14:6

2 Peter 1:1

Revelation 17:14

Satan is the god of this world. He is a liar, deceiver, and destroyer. Jesus is the King of all Kings. He is Lord of heaven and earth. He is the Light of the World. He is truth. And He came to save that which was lost.

5. In this chapter, I referred to James 4:7: "Resist the devil, and he will flee from you." What does it mean to flee? List some practical ways can you resist the Devil's lies that lead to fear.

6. a. Look at Psalm 91:4–11. What does trusting God provide for you?

b. What will not frighten you anymore when you trust God?

c. Who does He send to stand over you?

d. How does this passage affect you?

7. a. Think of your past fears. What fears have you overcome as a result of trusting God?

   b. How can this triumph encourage you to face your fears of today?

8. How has this chapter challenged you to get out of the safety of the boat and walk on water?

Chapter Three
Fashioned for Faith—Not Fear

Four and half years after I lost Porter, God brought a wonderful man into my life, and I remarried. While I know that Pat was God's choice for me, we don't always see eye to eye—mainly because we're opposites. Pat is compliant and levelheaded but somewhat fear-based and tight with his money—so tight he squeaks when he walks. I'm glad he's this way. I feel loved and protected knowing that he has carefully planned his funeral and has safely tucked away a life insurance policy in the lockbox at the bank. He wouldn't dare keep it at home. A raging tornado could strike, destroying our home and everything in it. Then what would we do? Silly me, those types of thoughts never occur to me. On the other hand, he is very humorous, relational, and loves a crowd. I like people too, but I also treasure my alone time. In contrast to Pat, I'm a free spirit who loves adventure but still gets lost driving in my hometown.

Family and friends are always teasing my husband about his conservative and cautious nature. One summer, our best friends joined us for a vacation at the beach. That was the year Pat attempted his first daring feat! Joined by our friends, we ventured with the kids into a water park. They had every kind of water ride imaginable.

The slides were the best feature of the park. Some whirled under and over before dumping you out into a pool of water. Others were enclosed with twists and turns that came unexpectedly in the dark. The most exciting slide dropped straight down and gave the thrill of free-falling. This slide was only for the daring.

Pat didn't want to go down the slide, but he had no choice. Both his son and his best friend challenged his manhood. Slowly, Pat climbed the tall stairs of the slide, looking back at me as if he were going off to war, never to be seen again. First, our son went down. "What a rush! That was awesome!" he boasted at the end of the ride. Our friend went next. "Let 'er rip!" he yelled on his way down. Then it was Pat's turn. Cautiously, he peered over the top of the slide, then took a few steps back.

"Come on, Dad. You can do it!" our son yelled.

Again Pat looked over the edge, but he still didn't get into position.

"Hey!" I called, egging him on. "Just in case, where did you say you put the key to the lockbox?"

That did it. He sat down, crossed his arms in front of his chest, leaned back, and away he flew! Instead of plunging to his death like he feared, he splashed safely at the bottom. Every tooth of his gigantic grin sparkled with pride. And why shouldn't he be proud? With courage, he had faced a fear that had tormented his mind, and the only dreadful result was that his bathing suit had ended up around his neck. He walked funny for the rest of the day, but I think it was worth it to him to have the sweet victory of conquering his fear.

Pat is the type of person who would like to check the bolts on the slide instead of blindly trusting its stability, but his faith wasn't in the slide. It was in God. Every step he climbed was a step of faith. He had to let go of his concern and trust God with the outcome, and that's just what he did.

Under God's Sheltering Wing

Instead of giving our concerns to God, many times we turn to false methods for overcoming fear. One false method is putting our confidence in self. This method teaches that the answer in within you. Find yourself, love yourself, and help yourself. You have the answer. You have the power. This idea may be a popular movement in Christianity today, but it's not biblical. The Bible doesn't focus on who we are, but whose we are and our identity in Christ. The answer to conquering fear isn't found in you; it's found in God. The right step toward freedom from fear is found in the words of the psalmist:

> It is better to take refuge in the LORD
> than to trust in man. (Ps. 118:8)

Those who trust in the Lord will be protected. There is safety in God. As long as we are safe in His care, we are free to enjoy life as God intended. Safety is not found in doing nothing or living in a bubble. It's found under the sheltering wings of God. He alone is our help and refuge.

Where do you run to find comfort from your anxieties and peace for your fear? If we are wise, you and I will run to the sheltering presence of God. Since we have fallen for Satan's lie that we can be our own god, we have become consumed with worry as we struggle to do what we were not created to do—be God. Any confidence we have quickly dissolves in the face of fear. Why? Because we know we are not enough. To find safety and shelter, you and I must learn to live in the presence of God again.

Adam and Eve had everything they could ever want or need. Best of all, they had friendship with God. They "heard the sound of the LORD God as he was walking in the garden in the cool of the day" (Gen. 3:8). How awesome to have God at their disposal! You and I can be just as fortunate. God's presence is still available to us today.

Will storms still come? No doubt. Nevertheless, living in God's presence is like taking shelter under an umbrella in the midst of a storm. While we can't stop the rain, we can keep from getting soaked with fear by taking shelter. Just as it makes sense to shelter ourselves from the rain, it makes even more sense for us to take cover under the sheltering wings of God during life's storms. For example, financial burdens may rain down upon us. We can stand in the storm, get drenched with fear, and possibly drown, or we can take cover under God's presence and not get wet with worry. Taking cover under God doesn't mean that our financial storm will suddenly dry up and the sun will come out. No, sometimes the storms of life can go on and on. Yet God's grace is sufficient. He is aware of our situation. Although the bills may pile up with no job in sight, under the wing of God we find strength to endure, peace under pressure, and a faith that anchors us until the wind and rain cease. The psalmist confirms this.

> He who dwells in the shelter of the Most High
> will rest in the shadow of the Almighty.
> I will say of the LORD, "He is my refuge and my fortress,

my God, in whom I trust."
Surely he will save you from the fowler's snare
and from the deadly pestilence.
He will cover you with his feathers,
and under his wings you will find refuge;
his faithfulness will be your shield and rampart.
(Ps. 91:1–4)

Living in the presence of God doesn't mean we will not encounter storms. It means that whether God provides a job or simply the strength to endure, we have a place to run and find rest in His sanctuary until the storm has passed.

Casting Your Cares

How do we get to this safe place in God where we run free and leave our anxious cares with Him? We follow Peter's advice in 1 Peter 5:7. He knew we would be concerned about the necessities of life. Even the most mature Christians today are apt to labor under the burden of personal concerns, family woes, and cares for the present, the future, themselves, others, and the church. Peter saw this anxious care as a heavy burden, and he gave us some wise counsel for dealing with it. Peter's advice is to *cast all our cares upon God.* We are to throw the cares that distract us, wound our bodies and souls, and lie heavily on our hearts upon the wise and gracious providence of God. You can do that because *"he cares for you"* (1 Peter 5:7, emphasis added). Isn't that amazing? You and I don't have to carry the burden of our worries. God is willing to release us from our cares and take our concerns upon Himself.

It's easy to cast my cares upon God. The hard part is not taking them back. When it appears to me that God is not paying attention to my needs, worry returns, and I feel the need to do something about it. When I was grieving for Porter, I suffered from colon attacks. It was how my body dealt with the stress it was under. I don't know if you've ever experienced a colon attack or have known someone who has, but they are agonizing. If you don't know any better, and I didn't, you'd think you were dying from colon cancer. The excruciating cramping in your stomach lasts for hours until it gives way to—well, let's just say more unbearable pain in the bathroom until sweet relief is achieved. Even though it's a painful experience, the worst part is not knowing where you'll be when the next attack occurs.

I assumed that casting my situation on God and asking Him to carry the burden meant that my stomach troubles would go away. When I gave it over to God, I expected to shed the burden of going to counseling once a week and having that extra bill to pay. But none of that ceased. I kept having colon attacks, which meant I still needed counseling for my grief. And while I hoped that the counselor would at least ease my debt, she instead raised her prices. *What was the point of giving my burden to God in the first place if He wasn't going to make it all go away?* I wondered.

The point is that when you and I cast our cares on God, we are recognizing that it's His responsibility to care for us—not ours. At first, the weight is lifted, but oftentimes God doesn't respond to our need as we think He should. Then we are quick to retrieve the burden. We forget that God is painting on a large canvas. He sees the big picture. We only see what's happening to us at the moment. God may allow events to come into our lives—good things and bad things, things that make sense and things that don't. Every one of these incidents serves as part of His plan for our lives. What you and I may think is harmful, God is using for our good—to bring us to completion in godly conduct and character. He will allow nothing to happen to us that isn't first filtered through His screen of protection. In other words, what won't destroy us, God uses to better us. Ultimate harm would be if God left us in the state we are in.

You and I have this promise in hard times: "We are hard pressed on every side, but not crushed; perplexed, but not in despair; persecuted, but not abandoned; struck down, but not destroyed" (2 Cor. 4:8–9).

God will not let our hardships destroy us. Though they may be tragic, He will use them for our good. You and I cast our worries on God, because it's His responsibility to give us what we need. As we trust Him with the bigger picture of our lives, the weight is lifted and peace washes over our anxieties.

Christ's comforting words remind me it's God's job to provide, and it's my job to seek the Provider:

> Therefore I say to you, do not worry about your life, what you will eat or what you will drink; nor about your body, what you will put on. Is not life more than food and the body more than clothing? Look at the birds of the air, for they neither sow nor reap nor gather into barns; yet your heavenly Father feeds them. Are you not of more value than they? Which of you by worrying can add one cubit to his stature? So why do you worry about clothing? Consider the lilies of the

field, how they grow: they neither toil nor spin; and yet I say to you that even Solomon in all his glory was not arrayed like one of these. Now if God so clothes the grass of the field, which today is, and tomorrow is thrown into the oven, will He not much more clothe you, O you of little faith? Therefore do not worry, saying, "What shall we eat?" or "What shall we drink?" or "What shall we wear?" For after all these things the Gentiles seek. For your heavenly Father knows that you need all these things. But seek first the kingdom of God and His righteousness, and all these things shall be added to you. (Matt. 6:25–33 NKJV)

What things will God add to our lives? Anything that you and I need! If that is truth, and it is, why worry?

Ecclesiastes 11:10 encourages us similarly: "So then, banish anxiety from your heart and cast off the troubles of your body, for youth and vigor are meaningless." This verse tells us to throw off our concerns and live fancy-free. We will not be young forever. Life is like a puff of smoke. Don't worry it away.

I like this philosophy. It reminds me of Scarlett O'Hara in the movie *Gone with the Wind.* Do you remember that classic? Whenever there was something to worry about, Scarlett always responded the same way. "Fiddly-dee. I can't think about that right now. I'll worry about that tomorrow." We'd do well to do the same. It is not our responsibility to control our circumstances; it's God's.

In the midst of our storm, Christ invites, "Come to me, all you who are weary and burdened, and I will give you rest. Take my yoke upon you and learn from me, for I am gentle and humble in heart, and you will find rest for your souls. For my yoke is easy and my burden is light" (Matt. 11:28–30). Carrying a heavy load of concerns can be a drag. It can cause us to grow tired, weary, discouraged, and afraid. That's why Christ offers us a helping hand. He may not choose to remove the burden, but He will carry the load.

Who's in Control?

One of the hardest things to do is to give up control of our lives and trust someone other than ourselves. Placing the very thing that worries us most into God's hands is scary. Why is that? Could it be that it's hard to trust someone you really don't know? It was for me.

I had been raised in church and had given my life to Christ at the young age of seven, but I never took time to really get to know God. Oh, I thought I knew Him. I could recite by heart the miraculous stories I grew up hearing. The problem was I had interpreted their meaning according to my own understanding—or what best fit my situation—instead of seeing the true meaning behind the stories. After Porter died, I had many anxieties about what and whom I believed. Even though I continued going to church, I didn't trust God anymore. He wasn't the God I thought I knew.

One day, after many invitations from my mother to attend Bible study, I agreed to go. Don't misunderstand. I didn't go because I wanted to know God or anything spiritual like that. I went because I wanted answers. I wanted to know why God had turned His back on me and allowed my husband to die. But a strange thing happened during that study. God never answered all my questions. Instead, He just showed me who He truly was—and He was enough.

After years of regularly attending Bible study, I began seeing things from God's perspective instead of mine. As my faith grew, it became easier for me to trust God with my fears. With fresh eyes I could now see what I didn't see before—God as He truly is. Are you doing the same thing I did? Have you conformed God to your way of thinking or do you really know Him as He truly is?

He's Got the Whole World in His Hands

My family and I love to vacation at the beach. As my husband and I sit digging our toes into the warm white sand, our children play in the emerald green salt water. The massive size of the ocean always reminds me that God is bigger and more wonderful than my mind can comprehend. I'm always compelled to quote Isaiah 40:12 while sitting on the beach:

> Who has measured the waters in the hollow of his hand,
> or with the breadth of his hand marked off the heavens?
> Who has held the dust of the earth in a basket,
> or weighed the mountains on the scales
> and the hills in a balance?

What a superb reminder of God's mighty power in the creation of the universe and galaxies. Even more amazing, He measured the span of them between His thumb and first finger. Hold those fingers up and look at their span for a moment. Now imagine God looking at the space between His thumb and first finger while saying, "I think I'll make the universe about that big." If that doesn't give you a picture of just how big our wondrous God is, think about this: He poured the oceans from the palm of His hand! Oh, friend, when I gaze upon a huge body of water that could swallow me up in an instant, and I realize that God, at some moment in time, held the entire ocean in the palm of His hand, it simply blows me away!

As I consider this truth, I find myself awestruck by the greatness and glory of our God. The Lord God is so gigantic that He knows every creature that lives in that great body of water. He sees every ship that sails its waves, and He even knows where the body of every person lost at sea lies. With a God this big, what could ever escape His attention? What need could we have that He cannot handle? Where could we go that we are not in His presence? What on earth, above the earth, in the earth, or below the earth can make us afraid? Certainly, we can place our trust in a God so big that even the ocean waves obey their boundaries.

And yet we doubt instead of having boundless faith in an unbound God. We live in fear instead of living carefree in the care of God. Let me ask you—what person or thing can compare to Him? Who or what is more stable than God? Is anything more powerful or glorious? Too often I forget the wonder of God even though all of creation declares His glory. I need to remind myself daily of His greatness. In doing so, all my fears tend to fade in the light of His presence.

Today will you take time to recall how great and magnificent He is? Do it again tomorrow and the next day too. See if you don't find yourself awestruck by the One so magnificent we can scarcely wrap our minds around the thought of Him. But, oh, how we need to try! It will do wonders for our faith and put to death our fears that smother our peace. Nothing gives me hope nor soothes my anxieties like meditating on the attributes of God. For what's impossible for a God who holds the whole world in His hands? Nothing. Absolutely nothing!

Genuine Faith

My faith in God didn't begin to grow until I started studying the Bible and discovering who He really is. In fact, I had misconceptions about God and about faith, and those ideas fed my fears. I have since learned that there is no power in faith alone. Faith is only as good as its object. Misplaced faith is dangerous. It's not faith that moves mountains, anyway; it's God. He is the object of our faith. People say all the time, "Just believe. Just have faith." I want to ask, "Believe what? Have faith in what?" Those are very important questions, because just believing is a faulty method for overcoming fear. Faith is not a principle of "name it and claim it." It's based on the person of Jesus Christ. If you and I put our faith in faith, then the Enemy will come along and tell us that our faith isn't good enough, strong enough, or real enough. This is Satan's most devilish work.

To have a strong, unshakable faith, I've found that I must look to "Jesus, the author and finisher of our faith" (Heb. 12:2 NKJV). Therefore, the way for you and me to have strong faith is to get to know God. When I spend time with God in His Word, I always catch a glimpse of who He is compared to who I am. Seeing God as He truly is reminds me that anything I do is insignificant compared to an all-knowing, all-powerful, and all-sufficient God. Faith comes by knowing God. The more I know Him, the more my faith grows and the easier it is to trust the Lord with my cares. Genuine faith is not what you and I profess to believe, but in whom we believe. If we want real, strong, mountain-moving faith, we must get to know God.

Live Like You Believe

The Bible is the best place to go to get to know God. In Hebrews 11:1, we find God's definition of faith: "Now faith is the substance of things hoped for, the evidence of things not seen" (NKJV). What is hope? Hope is the confidence that what God has promised will happen. If God said it, don't sweat it. He will do what He has promised. Hope provides me with this confidence: that God will forgive all my sins, He will renew me, He will give me peace in times of turmoil, He will heal my sickness and comfort my sorrows, He will fight for me, He will guide me, He will protect me, He will strengthen me, and He will care for me until all my fears are swallowed up by an undying faith in a God who is more than able to supply all my needs. Faith believes that God is real, and hope is the confidence that He'll do what He said He will do.

My eldest son once asked me how I can be so passionate about God and have such faith in Him. I told him that I started right where he was—afraid and in doubt. My faith grew as I chose to believe that God is real and that what He says in the Bible is real.

Satan is a liar. He is out to deceive us with fear and steal our faith, hope, joy, and peace. God's Word says that we have everything we need for life and godliness. Every precious promise is ours (2 Peter 1:3–4, paraphrased). We can say "yes and amen" to them all. How? By believing they are real. The choice is ours. It's this simple. If you and I believe prayer works, we will pray. If we believe God is working on our behalf, we will rest instead of worry; we'll have faith instead of fear. If we believe that we are blessed, anointed, and directed by His hand, we will live like it. Fear doubts God, but faith lives like God's unseen promises are true.

The word *substance* implies something sturdy underneath us. Faith is not walking around on eggshells in fear of having our stability pulled out from under us. Faith is standing on the firm foundation of Christ. Christ is our Rock on which we stand. What is our Rock made of? He's the Alpha and Omega, the Bread of Life, the High Priest, the Faithful One, the First and the Last, the Savior of the World, and the Good Shepherd. He's the Holy One, the Prince of Peace, the Lamb of God, the Light of the World, the Mediator, and the Messiah. He's the Passover Lamb, the Bridegroom, the Righteous One, the Resurrection and the Life, and He's the Son of the One and Only True and Living God. Jesus is the object of our faith and the one in whom we put our hope. If you know anyone who has better or higher credentials than these to put your faith in, let me know. I'll join you. Otherwise, decide today that you were not created for fear but for faith in God, who is more than sufficient for all your needs. When Satan tries to pull concerns down over your eyes of faith, simply declare God's sufficiency and watch Satan's fear tactics go up in smoke.

As children of God, we have the privilege of casting our worries on the Lord with strong confidence that He cares for us. Worry is unnecessary when our God is able and willing to bear our burdens for us. When you and I worry, we are denying the wisdom, love, and provision of God. We are saying to Him, "I really don't believe that You care for me." Worrying instead of handing our anxieties over to God says that we believe He is powerless to deliver us from whatever concerns us most. What is it that you honestly believe about God and His provision for you? I challenge you to pause here and determine the answer.

Living Aware of His Presence

I love Oswald Chambers' perspective on what should haunt us. He says we are to be haunted not by the concerns of this world, but by God. Not in a scary way, but in a conscious way. Not where we are merely thinking about God, but rather abiding with Him—always aware of His presence in our time of joy or need. Chambers illustrates his point by using the relationship between a mother and her child. "A child's consciousness is so mother-haunted that although the child is not consciously thinking of its mother, yet when calamity arises, the relationship that abides is that of the mother."[1]

If you're a parent, you know this to be true. When trouble comes, who does your child cry out for and expect to come running—none other than mom. The child may not be thinking about its mother as she plays. But when in need, the relationship that abides—the one that has shown care and provision—immediately comes to mind. I've seen this in my own children. My oldest son Mitch and his friend Jamie had spent the afternoon at our house watching movies up until it was time for Mitch to go to work. It wasn't ten minutes after they left the house that the phone rang.

"Mom, I just wrecked my car. I'm okay, but Jamie is hurt. We're just down the road from our house. Can you come?"

Can I come? What kind of question is that? I was already sitting in my car after he said the word "wrecked." I just needed to know what direction to go in.

It's one thing to hear that your child has been in a car accident, but it's another to witness the scene. The first thing I saw when I arrived was his car upside down and smashed between two trees like a pancake. An ambulance and fire truck were already at the site. Cars lined the road on each side and people came out of their homes to view the accident. Once my mind was able to take it all in, I realized that Mitch and his friend were nowhere in sight.

"WHERE ARE THEY?" I shouted as I turned in a circle, scoping the area for any sign of them. A paramedic took me by the arm and led me toward the ambulance. I felt my body go numb from fear of what I might find inside.

The first person I saw was Mitch. Our eyes met, and without exchanging words, I could tell he was scared but okay. Jamie, on the other hand, was strapped to a straight board with her back, neck, and head secured. Tears of concern filled my eyes.

"Jamie's hurt badly," Mitch said, as if I could fix it. At that moment, if I couldn't fix it, I was sure going to find someone who could. I bent down close to Jamie and took her hand in mine. "I'm here, sweetie. It's going to be okay," I said, trying to reassure us both. However, my motherly authority took over when Jamie shared her needs with me. I tried to relay them to the paramedic as calmly as I could.

"I can't breathe," Jamie whispered.

"SHE CAN'T BREATHE!" I shouted to the paramedic.

"I'm in pain," she begged.

"SHE'S IN PAIN!" I demanded. I felt as if I needed to lie down on the other side of the ambulance from the adrenalin rush surging through my body due to fear. Fortunately, we all survived the incident and arrived safely at the hospital. Mitch only received a few bumps and bruises. Jamie dislocated a few ribs, but after several weeks she too was as good as new.

My son may not have been thinking about me before the accident occurred, but immediately afterward he was aware of the person he needed most. That's because children are bonded to their parents by a love relationship that they don't necessarily think about, nor are they conscious of its existence. Yet in times of trouble, worry, or fear, the child instantly realizes the union. The same is true of our relationship with God.

I often take for granted the awesome privilege of being God's child. Like my son, I should be quick to call out to my heavenly Father for help. I need to run to God for comfort and reassurance instead of worrying myself to death. Often I do the opposite. I try to be the adult instead of the child, but I truly want to do better. I want to become so aware of God's abiding presence in my life that I fall asleep in His arms at night and awake to His presence in the morning. If God is our protective parent, and in Him we are safe, what is there to fear?

When everything had settled after the accident, Mitch could no longer hold in his fear. Burying his head in my chest, he burst into tears. It was his way of releasing his anxieties and casting them on me. Because I love my son, I gladly supported him in the midst of his pain. Wrapping my arms around Mitch, I reassured him that he was safe. As I held my son, the Spirit of God reminded me that,

> Even youths grow tired and weary,
> and young men stumble and fall;
> but those who hope in the LORD

> will renew their strength.
> They will soar on wings like eagles;
> they will run and not grow weary,
> they will walk and not be faint. (Isa. 40:30–31)

In the same way, our fears and worries should drive us into the safety of God's arms. Those who trust in Him have tremendous security. We find support in God's presence when we cast our cares on Him. No worry is too big for our Father to shoulder. Because of His great love for us, He gladly takes away our fears and quiets our hearts with peace.

Isaiah writes, "You will keep in perfect peace him whose mind is steadfast, because he trusts in you" (Isa. 26:3). In God's loving care, our spirit is renewed, and we know for certain there is no safer place on earth. The Lord picks us up out of our wrecked lives while we are still scared, and He comforts us. His rescue is certain and trustworthy.

The psalmist promises,

> Yes, because GOD's your refuge,
> the High God your very own home,
> Evil can't get close to you,
> harm can't get through the door.
> He ordered his angels
> to guard you wherever you go.
> If you stumble, they'll catch you;
> their job is to keep you from falling....
> "If you'll hold on to me for dear life," says GOD,

"I'll get you out of any trouble.

I'll give you the best of care

if you'll only get to know and trust me.

Call me and I'll answer, be at your side in bad times;

I'll rescue you, then throw you a party." (Ps. 91:9–12,

14–15 MSG)

Oh friend, God cares about all that concerns you, great and small. Nothing is too heavy for Him to bear. We should never stop relying on God to rescue us from the continual stream of worries and pressures in this life. In every pressured situation, we can be certain that God will remain true.

Bible Study: Know It—Stow It—Show It

I love to read church signs. Just one statement or thought on a church sign can preach a whole sermon. Recently, I read this one: "Worry looks around while faith looks up." Do you identify with that statement? I did.

1. In what ways do you try to find relief from your stress and anxiety?

2. Read Psalm 27:11, Psalm 86:11, and Colossians 1:9. List some benefits associated with knowing God and His ways.

3. Describe some of the blessings in your life that result from knowing God.

4. a. Read Philippians 3:4–8. What value does Paul place on knowing Christ?

   b. What value do you place on knowing Christ compared to your credentials, education, understanding, and abilities?

   c. How does your habitual behavior reflect this ranking of values?

   d. Have you ever thought about asking God to give you a greater desire to know Him? How might that benefit your faith and relinquish your fears?

5. a. Read Psalm 27:1–3. List four situations that could have caused David to fear.

   b. How can you apply each one of them to an experience in your own life?

c. How did David describe God?

d. How can these characteristics become an antidote to fear?

e. What two choices did David make, and on what did he base his confidence?

6. a. What fears are you facing right now?

b. In what ways does it help you to know that God cares?

7. From the following verses, describe the aspects of the Lord's character that make Him beautiful: Deuteronomy 3:24; Psalm 27:4, 34:8, 62:11–12; Isaiah 6:3; Nahum 1:7; Ephesians 2:4–5, 7; 1 John 4:16.

8. Your care is a burden that only faith can cast off. The advantage flowing from faith in God is a confident reliance on His goodness to provide for your every need. Does this advantage motivate you to trust God? Why or why not?

9. a. Read Psalm 27:5–12. Name at least five requests David
made to God as he poured out his heart in prayer.

   b. Are you seeking God in prayer? If so, what are you asking
Him to do?

10. a. Read Psalm 27:13–14. What enabled David to overcome
his fears?

   b. How can you apply what you've learned to your fearful
circumstances?

Chapter Four
The Pressure's On

Pressure—it's everywhere. It sneaks into every part of our lives. We have pressure in marriage, pressure to keep up and have more, and pressure to give our kids the latest gadgets. We even experience pressure for our time. No doubt about it, life today is stressful! And with stress comes fear. We fear losing it. We fear we won't be enough for our families. We fear failure. So we work longer and do more, all in the name of fear. Even though adding more is not the way to handle pressure, we do it anyway. Before we know it, our lives can resemble a three-ring circus as we try to juggle it all on top of a high wire. One of our greatest fears is that someone will discover the truth: We can't really juggle it all.

Think about your own life for a moment. What stressful circumstances are you facing that seem hopeless? Do you often feel like everything depends on you? Perhaps you fear that you won't measure up, or you fear what others think of you. Maybe you fear missing out on opportunities, so you stretch yourself thin, dipping your controlling fingers into every pot. Could it be that discontentment with life is adding undue stress?

Living under such stress is like living in constant terror of an intruder lurking in the darkness just waiting to attack. The intruder can bear many names: fear, pressure, stress, worry, control, old age, sickness, anxiety, Satan—anything that haunts us. Yes, you and I are being chased and hunted by these intruders. That's the bad news. The good news is that God has provided protection and provision when life presses in on us. Allow me to introduce you to God's bodyguards, Goodness and Mercy, in Psalm 23:

> The LORD is my shepherd;
> I shall not want.
> He makes me to lie down in green pastures;
> He leads me beside the still waters.
> He restores my soul;
> He leads me in the paths of righteousness
> For His name's sake.
>
> Yea, though I walk through the valley of the shadow of
>   death,
> I will fear no evil;
> For You are with me;
> Your rod and Your staff, they comfort me.
>
> You prepare a table before me in the presence of my
>   enemies;
> You anoint my head with oil;
> My cup runs over.

> Surely goodness and mercy shall follow me
> All the days of my life;
> And I will dwell in the house of the LORD
> Forever. (NKJV)

David wrote this psalm as praise to God for His faithfulness throughout David's life. It reflects David's confidence in "fearing no evil" because God is his shepherd who promises him "goodness and mercy" amidst the strains of life. I believe David named God's body-guards *Goodness* and *Mercy* to reflect their job description.

The dictionary describes *goodness* as a quality or personal virtue or the benefit that's derived from something. The biblical concept focuses on concrete experiences of what God has done and is doing in the lives of His people. The goodness of God is experienced in His creative work, saving acts, personal deliverance, and freedom from captivity to things such as fear, anxiety, pride, malice, and sin. God's goodness is extended in His name, His promises, His gifts, His provisions, and His providence in shaping personal and world events.

According to the dictionary, *mercy* means kindness or forgiveness to somebody you have power over or the easing of distress or pain. The biblical concept of the word *mercy* always involves helping those who are in need or distress. It's clear from these descriptions that Goodness and Mercy are God's aids that rush to our rescue when we are full of anxiety and in need.

We often mislabel Goodness and Mercy. We call them luck or coincidence. In God's economy, luck and coincidence don't exist. "Every desirable and beneficial gift comes out of heaven. The gifts are rivers of light cascading down from the Father of Light. There is nothing deceitful in God, nothing two-faced, nothing fickle" (James 1:17 MSG). Goodness and Mercy have many characteristics and come in many forms. You and I must believe that every benefit that comes our way is God's Goodness and Mercy following after us. As we anticipate their involvement and count on their help, God infuses us with fresh faith, fresh strength, and fresh peace.

When you're barely holding on, when you can't handle one more day of stress, when you can't parent those kids another minute, when you're about to blow—relying on God's Goodness and Mercy to show up will pacify your anxieties. They may not come when you want or the way you want, but God's provisions are always certain. That's a promise I've experienced in my own life, and you can too, because those whom God loves, He loves and defends to the end.

Me, Mother of the Year?

It wasn't until my youngest son entered kindergarten that I realized somewhere along the way I had adopted the Little Engine's motto for my life. Do you remember that childhood story? When faced with a challenge, the Little Engine would say, "I think I can, I think I can." That became my slogan as well. Whenever I was asked to be a room mom at school, teach a class at church, or leap tall buildings in a single bound, my response was always the same—"I think I can, I think I can"—until the day I discovered that I couldn't.

Tennessee kindergarteners follow a scattered schedule the first two weeks of school. Half the class attends one day and the rest come on the following day. It helps the children adjust. For me, it brought confusion.

On Tuesday I took my son to school, kissed him good-bye, and headed home to work. I was busy at the computer when the telephone interrupted my pace.

"Hello?"

"Mrs. Campbell, this is Parker's teacher. I was wondering who would be picking him up from school today."

Stunned that I had forgotten my child, I jumped in the car and raced to the school. As I pulled up to the sidewalk, he stood holding his teacher's hand with big ole crocodile tears in his eyes and REJECTION stamped across his heart. I took him home, apologized profusely, and made his favorite meal for dinner. I felt like the worst mother ever.

On Thursday we returned to school. All was going well until, once again, I was interrupted by the phone. I had forgotten to pick up my child not once, but twice in the same week! I didn't even take the time to put on my shoes before I sped to school on two wheels. This time I found my son standing on the sidewalk with the teacher's aide. As she helped Parker into the car and buckled his seatbelt, I tried explaining myself.

"You're not going to believe this, but I did the same thing earlier this week."

"Yeah, I know," the room mom replied bluntly.

It happened that quickly. In a single moment, I was labeled a "bad mother." Cracking under the pressure of a busy schedule left me feeling like a complete failure as a mother. Fear struck my heart as I wondered, "Is this what everyone will think of me? Worse yet, is this what my son thinks of me?"

Sometimes God lifts us from discouragement of failure in the most unexpected ways. A few weeks after the incident, someone from

ParentLife magazine called to announce that I had just been named Mother of the Year! What was the family's response? We laughed hysterically. Shocked, I kept repeating, "Me, Mother of the Year?" But it was my son's reaction that was the most humbling of all: "I bet if they came and lived with us for a while, they'd probably reconsider." Those were my thoughts exactly. In fact, I asked my husband, "How could I be given such a great and undeserved honor?" With wisdom he shared that maybe it was God's way of saying I'm doing better than I think.

My husband's comforting words helped me put things into perspective. God never said I had to be perfect. That was *my* expectation. He never said that I wouldn't make mistakes or a wrong decision every now and then. Again, that was my hope. I had assumed that the godly woman described in Proverbs 31 did everything right, and I was supposed to do likewise. With all of her great accomplishments, I never considered her not-so-good side.

It was never my intention to leave my son at school. I had allowed my life to get out of balance. By trying to do it all, juggling family and ministry, I had failed my son. God knew my heart was strained with guilt and grief. Through His Goodness and Mercy, God poured over my wounds His sustaining grace. The Mother of the Year award was the goodness of God delivering me from shame. It was as if God was saying to my heart, "Hang in there; don't worry. You're doing better than you think." God's display of mercy when I least expected it eased the pain of my distress. It enabled me to look past my failure and press ahead in renewed confidence.

From time to time, pressure may cause us to trip and fall, lose a title, or deflate our ego. God isn't concerned that you and I fall

down now and then. He just wants us to get up again. So He sends
Goodness and Mercy to aid us in the process.

Finding Balance in Contentment

Part of the process of overcoming stress-filled lives is when Goodness
and Mercy allow us to plummet to the ground as I did. I realize that
taking a dive doesn't seem like a good and merciful thing, but it is in
the long run. Sometimes the most merciful thing God can do is let
us fall. For some reason, it's when we're down among the mess we've
made that we can truly see our lives clearly. The incident with my
son showed me that my life needed balance. It's what every busy life
needs when our priorities are out of whack from trying to do all and
have all. Balance comes when I lay my to-do list before God and allow
Him to prioritize my life. My life doesn't belong to me as a Christian.
I shouldn't be the one ordering my days. When I do, my life becomes
unstable. When this happens, I've learned to do a quick review of my
life by using this acrostic on priorities given to me by a friend:

P - Pray. Ask God for wisdom. Ask Him to show you His priorities for this season of your life.

R - Review God's priorities for your life. Study God's Word to
determine His priorities for you as His child and as a woman.

I - Take *Inventory.* Examine the activities that consume your
time. Keep a time log for a week. Then ask hard questions. What are
my true priorities? Are they the right ones?

O - Order your schedule. Ask, "What is important?" Make the
hard choices based on God's priorities for your life.

R - Resist the "tyranny of the urgent." Don't let the urgent keep
you from focusing on the truly important.

I - Input from others. Seek input, counsel, and accountability from authorities, your husband, godly friends, and mentors.

T - Take advantage of the time God gives you. Don't waste time. Do all to the glory of God.

I - Identify time robbers. What saps your energy and robs your time? Activities, attitudes, distractions, interruptions?

E - Experience this season fully. Be all there in this season of life. Weep, rejoice, work hard, and celebrate with all your heart. Don't waste time living in the past or future.

S - Sabbaths. Take regular time-outs to refresh, regain perspective, reflect and evaluate, and reprioritize. Make adjustments accordingly.

Riches Will Make Me Happy!

Overextending ourselves only brings undue pressure to our lives. We busy ourselves in order to gain more, find acceptance among peers, land a better position, and gain riches of all kinds. We live under the illusion that having such riches is what makes a person complete, content, and deliriously happy. Author John Ortberg discusses the disconnect between material things and what makes a person truly happy:

> Yale theologian Miroslav Volf says that there are two kinds of richness in life: "richness of having" and "richness of being." … [Often] we seek richness of having, but what we really want is richness of being. We want to be grateful, joyful, content, free from anxiety, and generous. We scramble after richness of having because we think it will produce richness of being, but it does

not. ... We can have very little and yet be rich. A rich
soul experiences life differently. It experiences a sense
of *gratitude* for what it has received, rather than resent-
ment for what it hasn't gotten.[1]

Contentment and security are not found in titles or in the kind
of car we drive. The logo on a car only tells us what kind of car it
is—not who we are. True satisfaction in its purest form is found in
the wealth of who God is and the riches He graciously lavishes on us.
The psalmist says,

> Wealth and riches are in his house,
> and his righteousness endures forever. (Ps. 112:3)

When we constantly want more than God has given us, this
craving reflects a heart that is discontent. What we're really saying
to God is, "I'm not satisfied with what you have provided for me. I
want more." In wanting more, we place undue pressures on ourselves
in an attempt to get what God hasn't provided. Naturally, anxiety is
the result when we focus on anything other than God and His will
for our lives.

The Secret of Contentment

The pressure to have more and do more can lead us down paths we
never intended to follow. In our attempt to fill the vacuum of our
empty souls, we discover that external luxury is only a cheap sub-
stitution for spiritual wholeness. Paul, however, knew the secret of
finding contentment: "I am not saying this because I am in need,

for I have learned to be content whatever the circumstances. I know what it is to be in need, and I know what it is to have plenty. I have learned the secret of being content in any and every situation, whether well fed or hungry, whether living in plenty or in want. I can do everything through him who gives me strength" (Phil. 4:11–13).

Take note that Paul wrote these words in a high-stress situation as he sat in jail awaiting the verdict for a crime he didn't commit. I don't know if I could find contentment if I were in his sandals. I would probably strum my wooden cage with a rock, singing pitifully, "Nobody knows the trouble I've seen. Nobody knows my sorrow." Yet finding contentment doesn't mean we have to like our current situation, but it may require an appreciation for it.

Let me explain: Paul learned that we develop contentment when we are thankful for what God has provided, whether we like it or not. That's because peace isn't the absence of pressure. It's the presence of God and our attitude toward His provision in the midst of our stress. By expressing gratitude, Paul experienced richness of being, not having. The psalmist puts it this way: "Better the little that the righteous have than the wealth of many wicked" (Ps. 37:16). Indeed, it is better to be godly, content, and carefree while having little than to live under stress from the worries of riches.

You may be in a hard place right now, and you're longing for freedom. Maybe you're stuck with a stinking job; perhaps you have two of them! It may be that you live in a space too small for your family, and you hate it. You're not where you planned or hoped to be, and you certainly don't like it. You don't have to like it, but if you will choose to thank God for His provisions regardless of your feelings toward them, you'll experience the same contentment Paul encountered.

We must understand that being thankful doesn't mean that God will eventually remove us from our situation. He may; He may not. Rather, being appreciative sets us free from the desire to have and lets us rest in the riches of contentment. You and I shouldn't wish we were someplace else or with someone else. Our identity isn't in our bank account, social circle, or where we live; it's in God. When we reach a place of contentment, we don't need earthly riches galore. God becomes our greatest treasure. In Him we have everything we need.

God Has Gone Ahead of You

I didn't know it then, but even before Porter's accident, God already had a plan to care for me. I was far along in my pregnancy with my first child when my dad approached Porter and me with a heart-felt concern. With a new baby on the way, Dad advised us to invest in life insurance. It was a great idea, but we just couldn't afford it. Under the circumstances, Dad felt compelled to pay the premium until we could pay it ourselves. Porter accepted. Little did we know what the future held. Just two short weeks later, Porter tragically died. What would my son and I do now that our sole provision for food, shelter, and clothing was gone? The pressure was on as I tried to make sense of it all.

Sometimes God allows us to become pressured—not to terrify us or cause us undue pain but to purify our character. It's interesting that God uses pressure in our lives this way. In the same manner, pressure is what makes a diamond pretty, precious, and priceless. Diamonds are treasured stones that everybody desires. God wants you and me to become His treasured stones that shine with His glory. He uses the pressures in our lives to create in us a thing of rare beauty that everybody wants. When we allow the stress of life to purify our nature, we permit God to work for good and His glory.

When I became pregnant, Porter and I decided that I wouldn't work but would stay home with our son. It wasn't that we could afford for me to stay home. We simply chose to make sacrifices so I could be with our son. After Porter's death, things changed. I was under pressure to work. Like many, I needed to put my son in day care despite my wishes, and I had to do it quickly. I had no income.

During this time of terror and transition, family and friends brought food and diapers and paid some of my bills. Behind their efforts, Goodness and Mercy were protecting and providing for my son and me every step of the way. Overwhelmed with God's goodness, I sealed His acts of grace in my heart and allowed goodness to shape my character so I would in turn comfort others as I was then being comforted. Since then, God has provided many opportunities for me to be His hands of mercy.

Just when I thought God couldn't be any more gracious, it happened. It was nothing short of a miracle. It was Goodness and Mercy at their finest. Although the life insurance policy had only been signed two weeks before the accident and was still in the probation period, the company honored it. With that blessing, I was able to stay home with my son for a while longer.

It may be different for you. Goodness and Mercy may show up in a job offer that you weren't expecting. It may be as simple as someone buying you dinner or offering to babysit so you can have some time to yourself. Whatever the form, it is Goodness and Mercy showering you with care in your time of distress.

Acknowledging these acts of kindness, which flow from God's heart, builds our faith. Before we know it, our faith has become stronger than what we fear. I wonder in what ways Goodness and Mercy have shown up in your life recently just when you needed them most.

The Lord Is My Portion

Whatever your circumstance, God is aware of your needs and ready and willing to provide. It may not be much or what you hoped for, but it will be enough. This is the message found in 1 Kings 17. The land was suffering severe drought. God sent His prophet Elijah to a starving widow in order to save both of their lives. When Elijah arrived in Zarephath, he met the widow as she was gathering sticks to cook a final meal for herself and her son. A little oil and flour were the only resources she had left. When they were gone, so was her hope. She and her son would eat and prepare to die.

As the widow explained her despair to Elijah, he responded with orders from God: "Don't be afraid. Go home and do as you have said. But first make a small cake of bread for me from what you have and bring it to me, and then make something for yourself and your son" (1 Kings 17:13). Now get this—she obeyed without delay! I want to be a woman who obeys God the first time without argument. But let's be honest—sometimes it's hard to trust and obey when we have a need. In these situations, fear causes us to want to hoard our resources instead of sharing them. This widow was in great need and under greater stress to provide for her son. The famine had taken a toll on her meager rescores. In her mind, they were in a hopeless situation, and she was under stress to survive. If I were she, I probably would have used one of those sticks she gathered to make my point clear to Elijah. Tapping the stick against his chest, I would have said, "Look, Mister, no one gets one morsel of food around here until after my son has been fed! Do we understand each other or not?" Desperate times call for desperate actions, right? Wrong. Anxious times should cause us to look beyond ourselves to God for His provision.

That sounds good, but why is it so hard to do in times of stress? It's hard because when the pressure is on, we're not truly convinced that God will supply for all our needs for the days ahead. Yet we have this promise: "My God shall supply all your need according to His riches in glory by Christ Jesus" (Phil. 4:19 NKJV). God is our portion, our daily bread. If you need food, ask for it. If you need a job, ask Him to supply one. God wants to bless us, but often we forfeit His blessings because we don't ask. On the other hand, while God promises to meet our needs, He is not obligated to make us happy, healthy, middle-class citizens. What we can count on are His agents of Goodness and Mercy for deliverance and provision. Sometimes they show up in unexpected ways.

The Lord promised the widow that her food would not run out until the drought was over. Until it rained, they ate—not a fatted calf, but daily bread. As women of faith, we can laugh during times of hardship because God is our friend who declares, "Fear not, for I am with you; be not dismayed, for I am your God. I will strengthen you, yes, I will help you, I will uphold you with My righteous right hand" (Isa. 41:10 NKJV).

Everybody Needs Me!

What kind of pressured situations do you face? Are you stressed because you're unorganized and out of balance? Maybe it's the constant stress of trying to make ends meet. Is discontentment the villain that adds pressure to your life? For me, it varies. I feel the most pressure in being a wife and mother. It seems that everybody needs me—all at once!

The most stressful hour of the day for me is shortly after the kids come home from school. I call it the suicide hour. It's when all the chaos begins. While I'm home alone, I can be so holy. I don't have a problem in the world. As soon as my children come home from school, it's as if horns pop out of my head knocking my heavenly halo to the ground. There's so much to do—right now! And the first thing I do is panic. I panic because I just don't have enough of me to go around! Before I know it, I've blown my top. It's a shame really. Children shouldn't cause their parents to sin in this way. All kidding aside, I often feel the responsibility of caring for so many, and it drains me. I get worn out. David got tired too. His job was just as stressful as ours as he protected, guided, and tended to his sheep. How did David manage? He looked to his Good Shepherd for rest, and the Lord provided. David wrote, "He makes me to lie down in green pastures; He leads me beside the still waters. He restores my soul" (Ps. 23:2–3 NKJV).

It's important for us to rest, but do we? Can we? Perhaps you find it difficult to sleep at night because of the stress that plagues you. Sometimes I lie awake making my to-do list in my mind. In the morning, I wake up as tired as when I went to bed. The real problem is that I don't get enough sleep. The body needs at least eight sound hours of sleep a night, but the average person only gets six to seven hours of restless sleep and brags about it. When we have insomnia, we rely on faulty methods for rest such as drugs, sleeping aids, and nightcaps. Sometimes exhaustion takes over in the form of a cold or flu, and we're forced to rest. God has a better plan to relieve our stress.

God's Goodness and Mercy lead us to "lie down in green pastures" in order to revive emotionally, spiritually, and physically. Whenever I think of green pastures, I think of warm summer days when I was a little girl. My dad and I would lie down on the soft green grass in the yard. We didn't have a care in the world. We just rested and discussed the floating clouds hanging in the sky. Perhaps your green pasture is a quiet moment in your favorite chair, a walk on the beach, or curling up in bed with a good book.

Mercy reaches out to help by leading us by still waters whose tranquil flow invites us to relax. Oceans, rivers, and bubbling creeks are such cool, soothing places of refreshment. When I was a teenager and had pressure at home, stress at school, or trouble in my relationships, I'd walk down to the creek that flowed just beyond the dead-end street where I lived. It was a place I went to quiet my soul and refresh my mind. Often I'd sit on my favorite rock and read my Bible, because "the law of the LORD is perfect, reviving the soul" (Ps. 19:7). The creek was the perfect place to read God's prescription of truth that cured my doubts and fears. It wasn't long before my heart, mind, and soul were refreshed.

God never put us in charge of the world, just certain assignments. While the stress of our duties can deplete us, God has not left us empty. He desires to refill all of our dry places so we have supply for tomorrow. The secret is stealing away with Goodness and Mercy to places of God's unending rest.

When It Doesn't Turn Out Like I Planned

What you and I need to settle in our hearts today is that Goodness and Mercy will follow us into every stressful situation. Maybe your stress is the result of hurt. Listen, my friend, even in the darkest and most trying hour, God is near.

Brother Walter is an African-American pastor whose congregation partners with our all-white fellowship. Our two church families have grown to love and support one another. We believe that we are a beautiful vision on earth of what heaven looks like above. Not long ago, tragedy struck Brother Walter's home. Both his wife and daughter were ill and in the hospital at the same time. The husband in him longed to sit with his wife, while the daddy in him ached to care for his daughter. As he stood in the hallway between their two rooms, Brother Walter knew he couldn't physically be in two places at once. So he knelt down on his knees and entered the throne room of grace. Goodness and Mercy met him there and made provision. Family and friends poured into the hospital as representatives of God's hands and feet. They ministered comfort, support, and love to Brother Walter and his wife and daughter.

Sadly, Brother Walter lost his wife. Yet when things didn't turn out as he had hoped, he didn't fret or fear. He understood that while his wife was with God in heaven, God's Goodness and Mercy were also with him on earth sustaining him with strength, hope, and faith. Though his heart was breaking, Brother Walter stood before the church family and testified to the reality of God's Word: "Yea, though I walk through the valley of the shadow of death, I will fear no evil; for You are with me; Your rod and Your staff, they comfort me.... Surely goodness and mercy shall follow me all the days of my life" (Ps. 23:4, 6 NKJV). It was clear that God had come near in his darkest hour with comfort and strength he needed to endure.

Regardless of the road you travel—Lonely Lane, Brokenhearted Boulevard, or Poverty Parkway—Goodness and Mercy will follow after you. No heartbreak, no death, no betrayal, no rejection, no failure, no disappointment, and no evil can stop them. They will always come for you. They cannot fail you. They will never quit, never forget you, and never leave you.

More than in any other arena of life, our families are where you and I most need this confidence. Disappointment, stress, heartbreak, betrayal, death—any of these can beset not only our individual lives but our homes. Can we possibly live carefree in God's care in a world where not even our dearest loved ones are immune to harm? Yes, as we'll see next, we can.

Bible Study: Know It—Stow It—Show It

1. Look at how the widow in 1 Kings 17:7–16 encountered and responded to pressure. What is your usual response to stressful times?

2. Where do you feel the most pressure?
   In my job

   In my family

In my marriage

Elsewhere: _____

3. Read Psalm 23. In the first verse, what kind of shepherd is God?

4. Do you ever try to "shepherd" yourself or look to others for shepherding? Explain what you do.

5. How does placing trust in the Good Shepherd release the pressures in your life?

6. a. What does the phrase "I shall not want" mean to you?
   I will get everything I want.

   I'm a selfish person for wanting things.

   The Good Shepherd will make sure I lack nothing that I need.

   b. Why does this matter?

7. How does confidence in the Good Shepherd's reliability to meet your needs affect your fears?

8. Look back at verses 2 and 3 in Psalm 23, where the Good Shepherd leads us by still waters and down paths of righteousness.

   a. Describe a time when you needed clear direction in your life.

   b. What does God promise in Psalm 32:8?

   c. Why would God ever lead you down a hard path? What might He be trying to purify?

9. a. Review Psalm 23:4. Sometimes the valley of the shadow of death can mean a valley of darkness (suffering, uncertainty) much like the widow experienced in 1 Kings 17. When you're in a dark valley, does God seem close or far away?

   b. If God promises to always be with us, why do you think He allows us to feel His absence?

    c. According to Psalm 23:4, where is God's presence when
       we're in the darkness?

10. In verses 5–6, we meet God's bodyguards, Goodness and
    Mercy. Yet our being children of God doesn't prevent intrud-
    ers from invading our lives. Describe a time when Goodness
    and Mercy came to your rescue.

11. a. What is God's promise in verse 6?

    b. What will this promise do for you in your current
      situation?

12. How can thanking God ahead of time, anticipating His work
    in your situation, build your faith and disband your fears?

Chapter Five
Family Matters

Dear Lord, thank You for my three precious children. They are answers to my prayers. Each one was born beautiful and whole, with ten tiny fingers and toes. I was overwhelmed with love when I saw them. I didn't know my heart could love any one person the way I love my children. But Lord, I'm afraid. I'm so terrified for them to grow up in this rotten world of ours. I'm worried that they will give way to the temptations of the Enemy and that he might steal their lives. Oh, God, if You don't hear or answer another prayer of mine from this day on, please grant me this one. Give us a real Christian home where love abounds and each member grows to love You and serve You all the days of their lives. Help Pat and me to build a godly legacy that our children will embrace and pass on to their children. And may You bless my family and keep this agreement between us for generations to come, in Jesus' name.

I wrote this prayer in my journal many years ago when my children were small. While God continues to hear and answer all my prayers, He is still in the process of answering the one above. I've since learned that when I pray according to God's will, I can count on Him to answer, "Yes!"

Bible teacher Adrian Rogers once said that prayer starts in heaven.[1] The Holy Spirit finds the desire of God and puts that desire in our hearts. When we pray for what's been laid on our hearts, it goes right back to heaven in agreement with God's will. If your desire is to build a godly home free from fear and secure in the love of God, then that desire, like mine, started in heaven. And if it started in heaven, God will see it through, because He wants us to have successful families. If families are meant to succeed, then what's wrong with families today? As I write this book, it's evident that families are in trouble. Within one month it came to my attention that four teenagers attempted suicide and one succeeded. While I'm certain that teenagers somewhere attempt suicide almost every day, I found it disturbing that these four teens came from families I knew—good, churchgoing families. Something is terribly wrong!

A mom's most precious treasure is her family. I know. I'm a wife and mother. I can't think of anything in this world that I love more or would fight for more than my family. I'm sure you feel the same way. Yet we're not alone. Many influences in this world are also fighting for control of our families. Among many other things, television, the Internet, too many extracurricular activities, drugs, and music videos that promote sexual promiscuity among teens are all vying for our children's attention. It's enough to terrify any parent.

And we're not the only ones who are afraid. Our children have concerns too. A study at Iowa State University found the following prevalent fears in children:

During the school-age years, imaginary monsters disappear, but other fears begin to surface. School-age
children often have to deal with bullies, the fear of
rejection or embarrassment, and sometimes the reality
of being home alone after school. School-agers also are
aware of TV and news events that showcase murder,
drug abuse, kidnappings, and burglaries.[2]

We don't need to look at statistics to realize that families face
more pressure today than they ever have in the past. We live in a day
when we must become warriors for the family in order to conquer
the opposition we face. The battle is on!

Fortunately, we are not without hope. Psalm 127 provides us
with the tools we need to build a home that is protected, peaceful,
prosperous, and pleasing to the Lord:

> Unless the LORD builds the house,
> its builders labor in vain.
> Unless the LORD watches over the city,
> the watchmen stand guard in vain.
>
> In vain you rise early
> and stay up late,
> toiling for food to eat—
> for he grants sleep to those he loves.
>
> Sons are a heritage from the LORD,
> children a reward from him.

Like arrows in the hands of a warrior
are sons born in one's youth.

Blessed is the man
whose quiver is full of them.

They will not be put to shame
when they contend with their enemies in the gate.

As you can tell, it takes more than hammers and nails to build something of significance. If you and I want our homes and relationships to stand strong, we need God's wisdom, help, and blessing. We need the Master Builder. The best-laid house will fail unless God crowns it with success.

What kind of home are you building? Perhaps you're building the same kind of house that was built for you, or maybe you're determined to build something different. With the Master Builder's help, you can build a healthy, happy family.

Psalm 127 paints a wonderful picture of God's plan for building successful, worry-free families. Within the picture, we see that our responsibility is to be workers, watchmen, and warriors for our family. I had never seen this picture before until I heard speaker and author Nancy Leigh DeMoss teach Psalm 127 from the radio. I always knew that God was the Master Builder, but now I saw my role in partnership with God like never before. As you and I work according to the blueprint, God builds the family, keeps the family, and knits our hearts together.

Unless the Lord Build the House

When Pat and I purchased a piece of land and began building our home, it was very important to us to invite the Lord into this process. We desired that our home be built on a solid foundation, and what better foundation to build on than God's Word? Pat and I carefully chose Scripture verses, wrote them on strips of paper, and placed them inside the foundation of the house as it was being laid. We even chose a special Scripture that became our family's life verse. After we moved in, we invited family and friends over for a house blessing. A treasured friend led the ceremony by inviting our guests to pray for God's favor on every inch of our home.

Although my husband and I allowed the Master Builder to lay a firm foundation in the building of our home, we have experienced a few loose boards and stepped on a rusty nail every now and then. Usually, these things occur when my husband and I try to step in and do God's job. We let our anxieties about family get in the way of God's building work. Yet without the Master Builder, we have no blueprint to follow. God has a design for the home and every member of the family. When we let fear get in the way, it's like trying to build without the correct materials. It's only when we place our rusty hammers and saws in God's hands that He is able to do what we fail to do in our best human efforts.

Am I suggesting then that we lie back, let go, and let God do it all while we enjoy a leisurely life? No, I'm just saying that doing things in our own strength produces restlessness, not the rest we find when we work with God.

This is how it works. As we live our lives to the fullest, savoring all the joys and performing our duties in unworried dependence on God as our Master Builder, He guarantees us rest and blessings. Do you know any other contractor who warrants his work this way? The Master Builder guarantees rest if we don't vainly put our trust in our own efforts. Rather, we put full confidence in God's workings on behalf of our family. Our job is to walk in obedience to His will, seek His favor, and entrust our home to Him. Our trust is rewarded with this promise:

> Commit your way to the LORD;
> trust in him and he will do this:
> He will make your righteousness shine like the dawn,
> the justice of your cause like the noonday sun. (Ps. 37:5–6)

We cannot be led by our own wisdom. Trusting God to fill in the gaps, cover our flaws, and hold us together is the way to success. Without God, you and I wouldn't have the common sense to get out of bed. We wouldn't have the gifts or the intelligence to accomplish anything, nor would we have the ability to love or nurture our family as we should. With this in mind, we need not ever think we are sufficient in ourselves without His divine help and blessings. We should commit the building of our home to God and allow the Master Builder to do the work required. And yet how quickly we forget our need for God until trouble hits, and we are plagued with fear.

The Worker, Watchman, and the Warrior

A few years ago, Pat was offered an accounting job that included a big promotion. It was what he had been working for, praying for, and waiting to happen. However, once he settled into the new position, he had regrets. Not only did he have to learn a new job, but he also had to clean up the chaos someone else had left behind. On top of that, the company's financial status was hanging in limbo.

Pat's worries weighed heavily on his shoulders. He wanted to quit and ask for his old job back but felt he couldn't do it. As the provider for the family, Pat was deeply concerned about losing everything. He found it difficult to trust in God's promise:

> The LORD will guide you always;
> he will satisfy your needs in a sun-scorched land
> and will strengthen your frame.
> You will be like a well-watered garden,
> like a spring whose waters never fail. (Isa. 58:11)

Before I knew it, his concerns and anxieties became mine.

Looking back on this frightful time, I can't help but wonder what Pat and I were building into our children—faith or fear? As Christians, we should be the last people to be afraid of anything. We claim what Paul asks us in Romans 8:31—"If God is for us, who can be against us?"—but act otherwise when the foundation of our home is shaken. Our children shouldn't see fear in us. We can't say with our mouths that we trust God and contradict that trust with our actions. Our actions speak much louder than our words. So what does it tell our children when we're afraid to go to the doctor when we begin experiencing symptoms? What does it teach them when we constantly worry about who will move in next door or when we don't trust God to provide financially? We teach our children fear instead of faith when we try to live in our own strength instead of depending on God's ability. You and I are not meant to live that way. We are only required to do what we can and look to God for what we can't do.

It took Pat and me awhile to admit that our resources weren't limited to our own finances. We had God's unending wealth and provision available to us. It was foolish to attempt to get on our own what God was so willing to provide. How do we know when we're depending on God's strength and not our own? We know it when we can say in worrisome times, "This is not what I want, nor what I planned, but I trust You, Lord." In order to say that, we have to first determine in our heart and mind that we're going to trust God no matter what. We have to believe that He is faithful in all things. If you and I don't believe that He's faithful, we're not going to trust Him at all. Instead, we'll fret over our circumstances.

We also work at building our faith. By putting into practice what we learn from God's Word, we make knowledge a reality in our life. One step of trust leads to another until we find ourselves living care-free in His tender care. Sometimes it's necessary to repeat these steps when fear returns, pounding on our hearts. That's okay. Repeating the process is exercising faith, not fear.

In faith, Pat made an appointment to talk with his old boss. He knew it could go either way, but Pat also knew God was his ultimate provider. He would trust God's plan. Pat expressed his desire to return to his old job to his former boss. Surprisingly, they were thrilled to have him back. Pat resigned from the new job and resumed his old position. Looking back, Pat and I realized we delayed our peace by fearing the outcome. Once we got around to it, trusting God was so much easier. When my husband first switched jobs, we were overcome with worry and stress, but we realized that we couldn't be afraid and exercise faith at the same time. Our house couldn't have two builders. It was either us or God. Eventually, we gave up our restless cares and let God's peace flood our soul. We simply rested in God. What better place is there to be? Where are you today? Are you restless in your cares, or are you resting in His care?

To Guard or Not to Guard

The Lord builds the home, but the parents are the gatekeepers. A gatekeeper is like a watchman or overseer who monitors the family's activities and decides who and what is allowed access into the home. The gatekeeper should be aware of what is going on in the house and who is influencing the household. The watchman isn't afraid to let the kids' friends come over, because he (or she) decides who stays and who leaves, who comes back and who doesn't get to come back. A good gatekeeper also fearlessly protects the hearts and minds of the children by monitoring what they watch on TV and the Internet and what they listen to on their iPods. It's the watchman's unworried duty to monitor the home until all of the children can supervise themselves. As a trusted overseer, the watchman isn't afraid to trust the child again after the child has made a mistake, nor is the watchman afraid to let the child learn and grow through trial and error. Parents are not called to control their children. Controlling is a faulty method of parenting brought on by fear. You and I are to guard and guide our children by leaning on God as He, in turn, guards and guides us in all wisdom.

When to Guard

My daughter's relationship with her best friend went sour the year
they entered junior high school. Peyton came home from school
every afternoon in tears. She claimed that junior high school was
evil. When I inquired about how she came to this conclusion, she
shared with me that all her friends had turned mean. "It's as if they
were abducted by aliens over the summer, had their personalities
changed, and returned to earth," Peyton explained through her
sobs. She went on about how you had to wear the right clothes,
say the right thing, and be in the right group or you were considered a nobody. Suddenly, frightening memories of my own junior
high school years flashed through my mind. I knew exactly what
she was talking about. I had been there, bought the T-shirt, and
destroyed it. Realizing that teenagers at this age are full of hormones and trying to figure out their place in life, I gave Peyton's
friend the benefit of the doubt. However, the bullying continued.
Now I had a decision to make.

First, I had to determine whether my concerns for my daughter were necessary or if I was overreacting. Our emotions are not
always entirely wrong; they are just not entirely dependable—but
God's principles are dependable. I've learned that decisions based
on my feelings usually fall flat, while those based on God's Word
never fail.

After bringing my emotions and concerns before God in prayer,
I decided that Peyton and her friend needed a break. We nicely asked
Beth not to call the house for a while and informed her that Peyton
wouldn't be able to spend time with her on the weekends for a while
either. Peyton was devastated. My heart ached for her, yet I knew that

sometimes taking a stand is the only way to teach others how you want to be treated.

Once in a while, we would see Beth at the mall or while eating out. Peyton and I were always friendly. We made it a point to stop, acknowledge Beth, and say hi. Beth looked at us with confusion on her face. Then one day, the phone rang. The caller ID revealed that it was Beth calling. Peyton looked at me wide-eyed and asked, "Can I answer it?" I nodded. To my surprise, Peyton handed me the phone. Beth wanted to speak to me. She was calling to apologize for the way she had treated Peyton and asked if they could be friends again. Once again, they are BFFs (best friends forever).

As parents, it's our job to protect and guard our children. It's also our responsibility to teach our children how to protect themselves. One way you and I can teach our children to care for themselves is by showing them how to use God's Word as a handbook for decision-making.

When Peyton faces a new situation, she judges it by Philippians 4:8: "Whatever is true, whatever is noble, whatever is right, whatever is pure, whatever is lovely, whatever is admirable—if anything is excellent or praiseworthy—think about such things." Teaching Peyton to think like Christ provides her with a sure rule by which to measure all things. If a situation or a relationship isn't good, pure, or noble, she shouldn't get involved. Using the Word as a guide provides her with confidence to make good decisions when things are scary and uncertain. For Pat and me, guiding our children in this way eases both of our apprehensions about what they may face at school, church, and play. As you and I do our job, God is working behind the scenes doing His. And that's peace of mind.

When Not to Protect

Just as it's important for us to protect our children, we must be careful not to let fear cause us to overprotect. Take for instance, Parker, my relational child. He is very sensitive, kind, and compassionate. He doesn't like controversy. He likes to please. As wise worker, watchman, and warrior of the home, I feel it's my job to notice my children's strengths and weaknesses. Praying about my children's weaknesses helps puts my fears to rest. For Parker, I often ask God to thicken his thin skin.

God answered my prayer when Parker got Mrs. Locke as his fourth grade teacher. She was the teacher all parents and children dreaded. Mrs. Locke had a reputation for being overbearing, strict, and a bit on the strange side. Other parents were having their children removed from her class so fast it made my head spin. When one parent asked what we were going to do, I responded, "Trust God." As a Christian, I knew it wasn't right to judge this woman on hearsay, nor was I to react in fear. Also, I had done my job by praying for the right teacher. Now I had to trust God to answer my prayer.

It was tough. Parker cried every day after school. He was intimidated by her standards and terrified of not pleasing her. What did I do? I made an appointment to meet with Mrs. Locke. Parker felt certain that he would be moved out of her class by the next day. Unfortunately, I couldn't find anything wrong. She wasn't harming him in anyway. She was just tough on my sensitive little guy. I was torn about what to do. Seeing Parker so miserable and afraid made me want to rescue him from his fears, but I didn't have a good reason to justify that action. I turned to God and sought His guidance.

As the Master Builder of the home, God is guiding us as we guide our children. The truth of Psalm 32:8 brings such peace to my anxious heart when I don't know which direction to take. "I will instruct you and teach you in the way you should go," says the Lord to the psalmist. "I will guide you with My eye" (NKJV). If you're a parent, you know that you can guide your child with your eyes. One look from mother and the child knows exactly what do. In the same way, we don't have to fret about what to do. God is our counselor, available to us day or night. He is not only available, but He is also willing to guide us every step of the way, never taking His eye off us. As hard as it was to leave Parker in Mrs. Locke's room, I knew God was using her personality to strengthen his weaknesses.

Sometimes I want God to wave His magic wand and give my children what they need. That isn't the way God works. It's in our suffering that He matures us. It takes courage and faith to resist protecting my children from God's sharpening tool. Who wants their child to suffer? Not me and not you! Still, Parker needed to grow, and I needed to step out of God's way and let him grow.

Parker will encounter what I call "sandpaper people" (those who rub you the wrong way) his entire life. His dad and I used this opportunity to teach Parker how to handle and protect himself when facing a difficult person instead of living in fear. Assuring him that he was not going through this alone, I gave Parker a prayer and a promise to cling to: "Be strong and courageous. Do not be afraid or terrified because of [her], for the LORD your God goes with you; he will never leave you nor forsake you" (Deut. 31:6). We also discussed how important it was for him to evaluate each day by talking over his fears with his dad and me. My goal was to not cradle him as much as I longed to. That would only have left him helpless and afraid of meeting other strong personalities. My task was to build a healthy, mature adult that could live carefree in the midst of adversity.

Parker ended up learning more than reading, writing, and arithmetic in Mrs. Locke's class. I knew this because of his response later that summer when he was assigned to the meanest, toughest coach in the league. One day, after a hard baseball practice, I asked Parker how he was doing. He replied with confidence, "I'm okay." After a short pause, he added, "I think having Mrs. Locke as a teacher was God's way preparing me for Coach Bo, don't you?" I just smiled, and I think I saw God wink.

When to Trade Fear for Faith

Knowing when to protect my children and when to let them guard themselves can be difficult. What's harder is identifying fear-driven parenting that can destroy trust in the relationship between parent and child. Fear-based parenting can also prevent me from allowing my children to make mistakes and grow from them. My job, and yours, is to guide, nurture, and raise self-disciplined children who know how to live by faith, not fear. It isn't our duty to smother, control, or overprotect them. While some fears are valid and require parental action, others are not justified and need to be entrusted to God's care. Until I learn to seek and trust God's guidance, I won't be able to discern between the two. My decisions will be based on fear instead of faith. When this happens, the results can be dire.

My son Mitch is a born leader with his own ideas about things. Although submission is hard for him, he had always been respectful and obedient to our wishes as his parents. Then he turned eighteen and got a tattoo.

What did his dad and I do? We did what most parents do; we panicked and responded in fear. I worried that a tattoo would prevent him from getting a good job. I was concerned about what others would think. I was anxious about where he got the tattoo and if the equipment was sanitary enough. I was terribly disappointed and heartbroken, so I condemned his decision. In turn, Mitch packed his clothes and left home, taking my heart with him.

For two weeks I didn't know where he was or whom he was with. His dad and I left messages on his cell phone demanding that he return our calls, but he never did. Overwhelmed with fear, I turned to prayer. I was desperate for God's wisdom and guidance. My eyes were opened as I read, "Fathers [or mothers], do not exasperate your children; instead, bring them up in the training and instruction of the Lord" (Eph. 6:4). I had overreacted in fear. My disapproval and accusations only infuriated my son and caused him to flee. It was fear that caused me to mistrust and misjudge the situation. Fear-driven parenting can drive a child down the path we are so desperately trying to avoid. This is not God's plan.

In order to build a house of faith instead of fear, you and I must examine our fears before we act. We should evaluate our concerns with reasoning. I ask myself these three questions:

1. Will my child's decision bring harm to him/her or others?
2. Will my child's actions affect him/her spiritually?
3. Is the behavior age appropriate?

If our concerns cannot be validated, we need to cast our concerns on God and trust Him with the outcome. Sure, the child may end up stepping into a pit as a result of his choice, but it's the only way he'll learn to avoid the pit in the future.

My son, who I thought was made in my image, actually had dreams and a God-given purpose of his own. I had to let go of my own dreams, expectations, and fears and accept him as he was, tattoo and all. Once again, I phoned Mitch. This time, it was to ask his forgiveness. When the machine answered, I poured out my heart. "Mitch. It's Mom. I want you to know that no matter where you are, you'll always be in my heart. I don't care if you're tattooed from the top of your head to the bottom of your feet, I love you. Will you forgive me?" Mitch picked up the phone and the restoration of our relationship began.

Fear-driven parenting is never a good thing. Our children will make mistakes just as we do. The key is letting our children know we have faith in them even after they've made a mistake. That's the way the Master Builder works.

As you and I build our home according to God's plan, it's the Lord who keeps it. This confidence draws us away from our excessive works and anxious cares. Realizing our fragile state and our inability to secure the family by our own accomplishments shouldn't cause fear. It should point us toward the Faithful One who is able to keep our family. God bestows His blessing on those who trust Him and seek His favor and guidance. And what is that blessing? It's a household of faith built and kept by God.

Throughout the years, whenever terrifying troubles come our way, Pat and I have learned to count on the Scriptures that are tucked into the foundation of our home. Those concrete truths are the substance that provides us with a firm and steady base that we can rely on and rest in always.

A firm foundation of faith is key, whether we are building a family or rebuilding a broken heart. What if your foundation has been shaken by the betrayal of a family member, friend, or even God? Will you ever be able to trust, again? Yes, my friend, you can.

Bible Study: Know It—Stow It—Show It

1. Would you describe yourself as a faith-driven parent or a fear-driven parent? Why?

2. What are your children learning by your reactions to life? List specific situations.

Genesis 15 records the covenant that God made with Abram. A covenant is a pact or treaty, alliance or agreement, between two parties of equal or unequal authority. God's covenants were easy for the people to understand because they were based on the customary ways of forming contracts. Our God is a promise keeper. By looking at the covenant He made with Abram, you and I can be confident that God will, indeed, keep His guarantee as we trust Him to build our home.

3. In Genesis 15:1–5, what does God promise Abram?

4. In verse 7, why do you think God identified Himself in this
   way?

5. The covenant between God and Abram was built on the
   foundation of God's character. How is (or isn't) God's character being built into the foundation of your home?

6. What did Abram ask God in verse 8?

7. God confirmed His promise to Abram through the covenant.
   What questions do you have about God's guarantee for your
   family?

8. a. Continue reading Genesis 15:9–17. What do you think
      the smoking oven and flaming torch were that passed
      between the pieces?

   b. Does this verse mention anything about Abram passing
      through the pieces? Why do you suppose that's the case?

9. Read Jeremiah 34:18. What does this verse imply happens to people who don't keep their end of the covenant?

10. God alone passed through the pieces in Genesis 15 and so made it an unconditional covenant. If Abram had passed through, he would have been responsible to keep his half of the covenant. To ensure His plan, God alone took responsibility for the contract. This is the same thing that happened when Jesus alone went to the cross to seal our new covenant with God. How does knowing this give you rest concerning your family?

11. Did Abram have any responsibility? Look back at Genesis 15:6, 8–9.

12. In the Master Builder's guarantee for the family, what are His responsibilities compared to yours?

13. Read Genesis 15:18 and note that as of today, Israel still doesn't own all of the land God promised. Do you think He has forgotten His covenant? Why or why not?

Matthew Henry, a Bible commentator, observes, "God often keeps his people long in expectation of the comforts he designs for them, for the confirmation of their faith; but though answers of prayer, and the performance of promises, come slowly, yet they come surely."[3]

14. If you're struggling with fear today, how can you move from fear to faith?

Chapter Six
Learning to Trust Again

I was home alone when the phone rang. The person on the other end identified herself as a caseworker from Texas. I listened in disbelief as she informed me that my brother was missing and my nephew had been abandoned. Alarmed by the news, I listened intently as she explained her plan to hand my thirteen-year-old nephew, Tony, over to Social Services. I begged her to reconsider. She agreed to keep Tony one more night while I arranged for him to take a flight to our home the next morning.

As the caseworker continued with the details of my missing brother, my mind drifted back to a few weeks earlier when he was home visiting the family. My brother was about to finish college. He had money in the bank and plans to build a home for Tony and himself. What went wrong? Hanging up the phone, I sat motionless, staring off into space as my mind tried to make sense of it all. For years, my chemically dependent brother had disappeared periodically on one of his binges, but he had been doing well for quite a while now. The phone call came as a shock.

As the news sank in, I felt anguish for Tony, who had been discarded by his mother and left to be raised by a single father running from his own fears of rejection. Because of his dad's addiction, Tony had been abandoned again. The two people who should have loved and cared for him most did not. As a result, Tony's life is a mess. No matter what good he experiences in life, the fear of being rejected again causes him to sabotage any promise of success. Why should he trust anyone else? It's just too painful. Sadly, Tony's story is not an isolated case.

Alone, betrayed, and rejected. These words describe the worrisome emotions of millions each day—the old man who has no visitors, the single woman who fears she'll never marry but will be alone for the rest of her life. Drug addicts and alcoholics live in a dark world—alone, discarded, and afraid. Each person feels cheated in some way—abandoned and unwanted by family, friends, and even God. Perhaps this is the way you feel. The fear of being rejected has caused you to distrust God and others. If so, you don't have to live this way any longer. You can put away your tormenting fears and learn to trust again, because Jesus has experienced the same kind of rejection. "He came to His own, and His own did not receive Him" (John 1:11 NKJV). Jesus has been where you are, and He understands. We see this truth throughout the Bible.

A Change of Perspective

Mary, Martha, and their brother Lazarus often opened their home to Jesus and His disciples. You might say these three were in Jesus' inner circle of friends. As a part of the "in" crowd, Mary and Martha felt certain that Jesus would come to them when Lazarus took ill. They had seen Jesus heal and minister to complete strangers. Surely He'd come to those whom He loved. However, we see in John 11:4–6 that was not the case:

> When he heard [that Lazarus was dead], Jesus said, "This sickness will not end in death. No, it is for God's glory so that God's Son may be glorified through it." Jesus loved Martha and her sister and Lazarus. Yet when he heard that Lazarus was sick, he stayed where he was two more days.

Let's pause here for a moment. I don't know about you, but I find it very confusing that while Jesus loved His friends, He waited two more days before He came to their side. These verses appear to validate our fear of rejection. We think, "If Jesus easily rejected His friend Lazarus, then He can reject me, too."

When I lost Porter, I felt unloved and forgotten by God. I had trusted Him, believing, like most Christians, that since I was His child nothing bad would happen to me. When something bad did happen, I bought Satan's lie. "I knew it, God. I knew You really didn't love me!" This was the cry of my heart until I discovered truth. "Then you will know the truth, and the truth will set you free" (John 8:32). If we don't know the truth, the Enemy can easily keep you and me afraid and in bondage. I believed Satan's propaganda, and that caused me to doubt God. Moreover, I had loved and served God since I was seven years old. I was His girl. He had promised never to desert me, but now I was alone. How could God betray me? Many of us think this way at some point. We feel as if we have rights as a child of God. These were also Mary and Martha's thoughts.

I imagine as the sisters watched their brother grow weaker, they felt abandoned by Jesus. Like me, they had served Jesus with full devotion. They had opened their home and their hearts to Him. Not only that, but Lazarus was a wealthy man who supported Christ's ministry financially as well. Now, in their time of need, they were abandoned and without hope. Then their worst nightmare came true. Lazarus died. Do you know that hollow, helpless feeling that accompanies the pain of rejection, loss, and loneliness? I do. It may be the loss of your home, the loss of another pregnancy, or perhaps the loss of your virginity through rape or abuse. Maybe you've been rejected by your family or spouse or your parents gave you away as a child. You know the pain and fear that accompany rejection. Fear of pain tells you that trusting again is too risky. It's an ache that you long to bypass for the rest of your life. Yet you live in constant worry that it's lurking just around the corner everywhere you go and in everything you do.

The question on my mind and yours is the same as these two sisters' question. Where was Jesus? When He eventually arrived, walking down the road toward His friends' home, Martha ran out to meet Him. I imagine her beating her fist into His chest as she shouted with mixed emotions of fear and grief, "Where were You? If You had been here, my brother wouldn't have died!" Sound familiar? Have you ever asked God, "Where were You? Don't You care about me?" At the same time we're asking those questions, we dread the response. What if God doesn't care?

Well take a deep breath, friend, as you read this verse:

> The LORD your God is with you,
> he is mighty to save.

He will take great delight in you,

he will quiet you with his love,

he will rejoice over you with singing. (Zeph. 3:17)

Let that verse sink deep into your heart. God cares for you greatly. We are His joy and delight. Yes, yes, a thousand times, yes, He loves you and me so much that the mere thought of us causes Him to sing and dance! I know it doesn't always appear like it. That's because our perspective is limited by our circumstances. I assure you, God knows exactly what He's doing in your life and mine, and it's always based on love. I've found that when I'm overcome with fear, I'm not really looking for answers but for the assurance that God is near, that He's in control, and that He cares about me and my circumstances. God does care.

You may be in the winter of your life, and your family has grown and gone. They say they love you, but they never come to visit. Perhaps you're young and single, and your greatest fear is not finding someone who will love you. You wonder, "What if no one finds me lovable?" The truth is that while others might withhold love from you, God never has, and He never will.

When I was a teenager, my sister and I used to watch those black-and-white films where Dean Martin would serenade his beloved below her windowsill. I would never admit it to my sister, but secretly I'd dream about that happening to me. I just knew that one day some guy would be so in love with me that he'd serenade me outside my window. Well, guess what? It never happened. But that's okay. You know why? Because God Almighty sings and dances over me!

The next time you feel unloved, alone, and rejected, recall this truth. Say out loud, "God does love me. I am His joy and delight so much so that He sings and He dances over me." Then, ask God for a dance, and let Him reassure you of His love.

God Means It for Good

Beyond a doubt, Jacob loved his son Joseph. In reading Joseph's story recorded in Genesis 37—50, I couldn't help but think Joseph would make a great guest on *Oprah*. He was coddled by his father, despised and betrayed by his brothers, falsely accused of rape and thrown into jail, had the gift of interpretation, was elevated from prisoner to second in command, and saved all of Egypt from famine. What a life! Wouldn't that make a great talk show story?

Joseph came into this world an innocent child. He didn't ask to be born. Joseph, like any of us, deserved to be cared for, loved, and nurtured by his parents. I recall my nephew Tony once saying, "I deserved to be cared for instead of having to look after myself." Perhaps you can identify. Or maybe you can identify with Joseph's brothers, who also deserved their father's love, but they had to settle for being second best after Joseph. Their father's rejection caused terrible sibling rivalry until the day Joseph's brothers threw him into a pit. Is that where you are right now, friend? Have you been betrayed and thrown into the pit of rejection? Don't fear. You're not lost. God has not abandoned you. He knows your whereabouts, and He has a good plan for you just as He did for Joseph.

While Joseph's brothers were eating supper, the opportunity of a lifetime arose. A caravan of Midianites passed their camp on their way to Egypt. Seizing the opportunity, the brothers sold Joseph as a slave for twenty pieces of silver. In U.S. money, that amounts to $1.28. However, several years later, during a life-threatening drought, Joseph's brothers traveled to Egypt to buy grain. It was their brother Joseph who had foretold the drought and prepared Egypt for survival. Many came from all over to buy grain, and so did Joseph's brothers. By now Joseph had been promoted to second in command in Egypt. In his powerful position, Joseph could have taken revenge on his brothers for betraying him. Instead, he chose to forgive them and reunite with his family. As his brothers bowed before Joseph in fear for their lives, Joseph said, "But as for you, you meant evil against me; but God meant it for good, in order to bring it about as it is this day, to save many people alive" (Gen. 50:20 NKJV). This verse is often compared to Romans 8:28, "And we know that in all things God works for the good of those who love him, who have been called according to his purpose."

When you, I, and Tony can let down those walls of fear and trust others again—especially God—we'll find healing and restoration just as Joseph did. Instead, we often want to cling to the belief that denial protects us from the pain and fear that comes with rejection, but the reality is that it only allows our wounds and fears to fester and grow. God has so much more for us. What was meant for evil in our lives, He wants to use for our good. The choice is ours. We can focus on the worries, burdens, and fears of our limited experience and miss the joy that can be ours or, like Joseph, we can take the risk, venture out, and truly believe that God has a plan. Not just any kind of plan, but one that is so good we'll be able to look back and say it was worth it.

Worth It All

While others may reject us, you and I need not fear God's rejection. As I began to understand that God had not left me but rather was in the pit with me, I started to see a deeper truth. Bad things are going to happen to me while I'm on earth. Usually, they are the result of living in this fallen, sin-sick world. While death, sickness, and abuse were not part of God's original plan, He may allow me to go through these things. It's not to cause me undue pain or fear, but rather it's to accomplish spiritual growth. Sometimes what God allows shakes us to the core, but He never intends to terrify us. It may not be pleasant for a while, but in the end we'll find it's worth every heartache and every worry if we trust Him.

A few years ago, my neighbor was bitten by a brown recluse spider. She was a diabetic, and the poison attacked the weakest part of her body—her eyes. After many surgeries, doctors were able to freeze Kathy's eye loss so that she doesn't have to live completely in the dark.

At first Kathy went through all sorts of emotions. She questioned God's love and protection. She wondered, "Why me?" and felt afraid and sorry for herself most of the time. Her husband, on the other hand, was supportive and full of faith, reassuring her. His confidence in God surprised Kathy. For over fifteen years, Kathy had been going to church alone while praying for Don, who had fallen away from God. Now it appeared that Don had more faith than she did. Kathy decided to hang up her worries and trust God.

Since Kathy couldn't drive, Don took her to and from church every Sunday. On the ride home, Kathy shared how nice the service was and how loving the people were. One Sunday morning, Kathy noticed that Don was all dressed up. When Kathy asked where he was going, Don replied that he was going to church. Don not only went to church that day, but he rededicated his life to the Lord and was baptized. Suddenly, it all became clear for Kathy. "My suffering was nothing like what Christ suffered for my salvation, but I would go through all my pain again knowing now that God was using it to bring my sweet husband to Him," Kathy shared with great joy.

Kathy believed she saw what God was up to, but sometimes it's hard to see God at work in our circumstances until decades later. In other situations, we may never see or understand God's plan. The Lord never promised that our journey would be easy. Suffering is real in our fallen world. While we would rather experience comfort and pleasure, no one is exempt from pain—not even Christ.

Peter suggests that our sufferings can come either when we do evil or when we do good: "It is better, if it is God's will, to suffer for doing good than for doing evil" (1 Peter 3:17). It's not always our fault! Our pain can be the result of our own rebellion or the rebellion of others. It can also be the product of a close relationship with God in which we are persecuted for our faith. Sometimes it simply comes from living in a fallen world. The only way to see worth in our pain is to realize it has purpose. Though we despise suffering, it educates us, transforms us, allows us to share in the inheritance of Christ, and gives us a ministry of compassion for others who suffer. This is God's promise. He is faithful in using every situation for our good. Again, it's not just any good, but the kind of good that causes us to look back—whether here on earth or in eternity— and say like Kathy, "It was all worth it. Look what our good and gracious Lord has done!"

Jesus Knows

It still may appear to you that God is coldhearted in His ways, but remember that Jesus wept with Mary and Martha:

> When Jesus saw [Mary] weeping, and the Jews who
> had come along with her also weeping, he was deeply
> moved in spirit and troubled. "Where have you laid
> him?" he asked.
>   "Come and see, Lord," they replied.
>   Jesus wept. (John 11:33–35)

When you and I hurt, Jesus hurts. Our pain moves Him because He cares about us. Even though Jesus was working toward a higher purpose in this situation, He was not emotionally detached from their pain. Likewise, just as Christ grieved alongside Mary and Martha, comforting their distress and hurts, He also grieves alongside you and me. The psalmist tells us,

> He heals the brokenhearted
> and binds up their wounds. (Ps. 147:3)

Jesus knows our hurts both intellectually and emotionally. The Hebrew word for "know" is *yada*. It speaks of a deep emotional experience and bonding between two people, when one is truly able to feel the emotions of the other. This is our God, who is able to say He knows the sufferings of His people. We do not have a High Priest who doesn't know what suffering, fear, and abandonment are. It comforts me to know that God is aware of my anxieties. I also find it comforting to know that during His ministry on earth, Jesus experienced times of great anxiety too.

When Christ was in the garden of Gethsemane, He endured great pain as He faced His fate of death on a cross. Never once did

He thank God for the pain. He didn't rejoice in His fear, nor was He grateful for His suffering. No, He experienced deep sorrow, desertion, and fear as you and I have. Christ endured because He knew that God's love was the source of His strength. Jesus could trust God regardless of His circumstances. I wonder if Jesus quoted Isaiah 54:10 many times during His suffering: "'Though the mountains be shaken and the hills be removed, yet my unfailing love for you will not be shaken nor my covenant of peace be removed,' says the LORD, who has compassion on you." Hear this and allow the truth of it to warm your heart and calm your fears: God knows. He's been there, and He is there still.

Learning to Trust Again

We've established that Jesus loves us just as He loved Mary, Martha, and Lazarus. He cares about all that concerns us. While He allows certain things in our lives for our own good and for His glory, it doesn't change the facts. Lazarus was still dead and so was my husband, Porter. I can't tell you how many times I struggled with trusting God again after Porter's death. I mean, He's God. He could have saved Porter. At the time, I couldn't see past my fears. Therefore, I couldn't see God, let alone trust Him.

Jesus told Martha that she would see the glory of God if she believed. "Did I not tell you that if you believed, you would see the glory of God?" (John 11:40). Did you catch that? Believing is seeing. If you and I will choose faith over fear, we will see the glory of God turn our worries into life and blessings.

That sounds great, but after you've been betrayed by someone, it's only natural to want them to prove themselves first before you trust again. The same is true when it comes to trusting God. If He would make the first move, then you'd believe, right? Wrong. God requires us to believe first, and then He moves on our behalf.

Author and speaker Louie Giglio says this about trusting God:

> Our trust in another person has to start somewhere other than in that person's size and strength. It starts in their proven character over time. But you and I can trust our God with our lives for that very reason. God is not only big enough to make the universe; He has created a universe that is breathtakingly beautiful, intricately ordered, scientifically dependable, the stuff of architectural genius. The universe itself declares to us that God is beauty personified, that He is organized and detail-oriented, that He is reliable and trustworthy, that He is genius defined. It's not just that God made the world that causes us to trust Him—it's the kind of world He made.[1]

Believing is easy when we open our eyes and see the glorious evidence of His faithfulness all around us. As the psalmist writes, "The heavens declare the glory of God; the skies proclaim the work of his hands" (Ps. 19:1).

Jesus' goal for Mary and Martha was "that they might believe." As Mary and Martha exercised their faith, they witnessed the glory of God raising their brother from the dead. Their fears vanished, and their faith was restored. If you and I want to exchange our fear for faith, we must believe that Christ can bring forth new life from the dead places of our hearts marked by pain.

When God Trusted Us

How are you doing at this point? Perhaps you're thinking, "My faith just isn't that strong." You want to believe, but you're too afraid. I assure you that you're not alone. For example, in Mark 9, a person just like you and me struggled with his faith. He cried out to Jesus, "Help me overcome my unbelief!" (Mark 9:24). You see, we can ask God to increase our faith. My faith increased greatly the day I realized how much God trusted mankind. "For God so loved the world that He gave His only begotten Son, that whoever believes in Him should not perish but have everlasting life" (John 3:16 NKJV).

As I came across this familiar verse, a new bud of faith was birthed in my heart. God sent His Son to earth as a helpless baby to be cared for by sinful humans. Just think about that for a minute. Jesus took off His robe of righteousness, laid aside His royal crown, and gave up His heavenly title to come to a world full of darkness and sin. He came as a baby, dependent and weak just like us. The truth that grabbed my heart and changed it forever was this: If God can trust you and me, then we can certainly trust Him. To think that God entrusted His Son to a broken, fallen, mixed-up world shouts one thing: Your parents may not be faithful; your spouse may not be faithful; your children, your friend, your boss, or even you may not be entirely faithful—but your God is always faithful! "Know therefore that the LORD your God is God; he is the faithful God" (Deut. 7:9). If placing His Son in the hands of a scared teenage girl isn't trust, I don't know what is. But choosing to stand on this truth is a step toward fearless living.

From Tragedy to Triumph

We will always have things in our life that we fear and can't explain—being the bridesmaid but never the bride, the child of a parent who chooses alcohol over family, the lonely divorcée, the empty nester, the throwaway child. On the other hand, God loves to turn tragedy into triumph. The greatest tragedy for my nephew Tony is not his parents' betrayal. The real tragedy is that he can't see any immediate good in his situation. Therefore, he continues to struggle with fear. He is missing out on the life God intends for him.

What about you? When you think of that someone who betrayed you, does your blood begin to boil? Are you justified in being angry? Anger is a symptom of your hurt, and both your anger and your hurt are fueling your fears. I know. I was hurt and angry with God when I shook my fist in His face. He had only one word to say on the matter: "Forgive." That means you and I have only two choices. We can either die in our fear of rejection, or like Joseph we can trust again through forgiveness.

Some commentaries say that Joseph was a picture of Christ. Like Christ, Joseph forgave his brothers' offense and erased all he held against them. Jesus did the same for you and me. In Colossians 2:14, the apostle Paul says Jesus "wiped out the handwriting of requirements that was against us, which was contrary to us. And He has taken it out of the way, having nailed it to the cross" (NKJV).

I owe God a debt I cannot pay, because I violated His law. But through Christ's sacrificial death on the cross, God has totally erased my debt, and He's made my forgiveness complete. That's the way He challenges me to forgive others—because I have been forgiven much. He doesn't ask me to develop a case of amnesia in which all memory of how others have hurt me is erased. He simply asks me to let Him open the wound and drain it of its poison. You and I have to be willing to remove the stones of fear, rejection, doubt, pride, anger, and hurt that have hardened our hearts. This is what Jesus told Martha to do. In order to experience life—resurrection life—she had to remove the stone.

> So they took away the stone.… Jesus called in a loud voice, "Lazarus, come out!" The dead man came out, his hands and feet wrapped with strips of linen, and a cloth around his face.
> Jesus said to them, "Take off the grave clothes and let him go." (John 11:41–44)

These verses are often shared at graveside services. I thought it was appropriate for the pastor to share them at Porter's gravesite, since he had been burned beyond recognition and his body wrapped and bound in bandages. Once Porter had crossed over into eternity, he had no more pain or fear—just peace. It was right for the pastor to say, "Loose him and set him free," for he was free indeed.

If Mary and Martha had not removed the stone, there would have been no lesson of good, no glory for God, no ability to move forward in comforting others, and no peace. No doubt you are reading this book in search of freedom from your fears. I want to assure you, it's God's desire that you be loosed and set free from all worry.

The first step is a changed perspective. You and I must trust that our situation will be worth what we gain in the end. We must let the love of God fill our empty places and wash away all our doubts. We must remove the stones that harden our hearts and keep us in bondage. Only then will we hear from heaven's balcony a heavenly voice proclaiming, "Loose her and set her free."

The kind of freedom Christ longs to provide covers more than the fear of loneliness, betrayal, and rejection. It also includes the concerns we have about current world issues. We don't have to speculate about the worst-case scenario of our day and how it may affect our lives. When you and I are secure in God's provision, there's no situation that can destroy us.

Bible Study: Know It—Stow It—Show It

1. Are you mostly likely to view your concerns from your perspective or from God's vantage point? Give an example.

2. How can looking at your circumstances from God's perspective lessen your anxieties?

3. "'Lord,' Martha said to Jesus, 'if you had been here, my brother would not have died'" (John 11:21). What tone of voice do you think Martha had when addressing Jesus in this verse?
Angry

Hurt

Humble

Timid

Confused

Other (name it)

4. Have you ever told God you were scared and angry? If so, what was His response?

5. Read Hebrews 4:14–15. What kind of High Priest is Jesus?

6. How does knowing that you have a God who understands what you're feeling comfort your worries? (Or if it doesn't comfort you, talk about why not.)

7. What stones do you need to remove?

Fear

Anger

Doubt

Pride

Unbelief

Other (name it)

8. In what areas of your life has Jesus helped you grow and conquer your fears of abandonment, rejection, or loneliness?

9. a. Read Genesis 37:18–33. What fears do you think Joseph
      had when his brothers threw him into the pit?

   b. In what ways do you identify with those fears?

   c. We are told continually that God's favor was on Joseph,
      and Joseph was aware of God's blessings on his life.
      According to Genesis 39:3–21, did Joseph lose God's
      favor? How can you tell?

d. Why would God allow Joseph to be thrown into jail?

e. What was Joseph's reaction to being in jail? Did he fear each day, wondering where God was, or did he trust that God's presence was still with him?

f. How can you apply what you've learned about Joseph as you battle your own fears or lack of faith?

10. "You intended to harm me, but God intended it for good to accomplish what is now being done, the saving of many lives" (Gen. 50:20). According to this verse, did Joseph think the things he endured as a result of his brothers' betrayal were worth it? Why or why not?

11. Do you need to forgive someone for betraying you? If so, who?

12. Are you ready to exchange your fear for faith and trust again? Why or why not?

13. In what way did God challenge or speak to you in this
    chapter?

Chapter Seven
What's the Worst That Could Happen?

My youngest son is a Curious George. He loves to ask, "Why?" As bothersome as that can be at times, I'm thankful that he has an inquisitive mind. You can almost see the wheels of knowledge turning in his head as he hangs on every word that gives light to his questions. One day while we were driving in the car, Parker asked, "Mom, what's the worst thing that can happen?"

I knew exactly where this question originated. The night before, our family had cuddled together in the hallway of our home with flashlights, blankets, and the cell phone, waiting for a furious storm to pass. Parker had many questions that night, too: "What if the tornado hits our house? What if the roof falls in and chops off my leg? What if we're all killed by the tornado, even the dog?" he had cried. I thought we had been successful in calming his fears. Evidently, I was wrong. Parker still needed to know the worst-possible-case scenario.

You may have a similar question—and with good reason. Disaster is all around us. It appears we are living in a new era, a time filled with darkness, mystery, and fear. Terrorists seeking nuclear bombs, global warming, widespread epidemics, rising crime rates, social instability—the list is long. It seems we really do have cause to fear. Or do we? Jesus told us that we can expect wars, famine, and uncertain times—and then the end will come. If that's the case, then what is the worst thing that could happen to us? Is it a failing economy? Is it global warming? Or is it the end of time?

Nothing New under the Sun

These are the same kinds of questions that I imagine people asked in Noah's day. Noah lived in a world not too different from our contemporary society. Jesus described that civilization as "eating and drinking, marrying and giving in marriage" (Matt. 24:38). From Noah's time up until our time, not much has changed. Despite the presence of evil, people are living everyday life as usual.

The biblical account of Noah's day suggests that, like all societies, it was permeated with evil, and this afflicted the heart of God. "The LORD was grieved that he had made man on the earth, and his heart was filled with pain" (Gen. 6:6). The Lord said to Noah, "I am going to bring floodwaters on the earth to destroy all life under the heavens, every creature that has the breath of life in it. Everything on earth will perish" (Gen. 6:17).

Yet in the midst of evil, "Noah found grace in the eyes of the LORD" (Gen. 6:8 NKJV). He was a man of faith, and it showed in his works. Noah preached to the people about the judgment of God, and his lifestyle of faith gave credibility to his message. If you and I want our testimonies to have credibility, we must live a lifestyle of faith, not fear, in both our private and public lives. Just think what your faith could do in the lives of others. Through Noah, God planned to salvage a part of the world. Although Noah's preaching rendered no fruit, God still provided a way of salvation. He told Noah to build an ark.

Building the ark hundreds of miles away from the sea had to be the greatest expression of Noah's faith. I can only imagine the ridicule Noah went through while building the ark. Day and night he dodged the cruel jokes the mockers threw at him, while in his mind he must have questioned, "Why, God? Why are you making a fool of me? You could at least send one rain cloud overhead."

We fear mockery. No one wants to be different or stand out as a weirdo. And nothing says "weird" like a man on a huge boat shouting "Flood!" on a bright, sunny day, hundreds of miles from any large body of water. But as strange as things seemed, Noah believed God. As wicked and unpleasant as times were, Noah knew something more horrible was coming, and the ark was God's provision of salvation.

The troubles in our world today are not new. They may come upon us in a new way, but they are still the same temptations, trials, and troubles that have always confronted society since the garden of Eden. Every day the newspaper, radio, Internet, and television give evidence to the fact that our world is evil. Anger, pride, doubt, fear, despair, abuse, war, sickness, and death haunt every country. Each person in some way has tasted the bitterness of sorrow and tragedy. In spite of all that, this was never God's plan. In His original blueprint, God didn't design disease, exploitation, uncertainty, combat, gloom, misery, or death. These are all results of living in a fallen, broken, sin-sick world. God said everything He made was "good" (Gen. 1:31). Then sin entered in, and we've been a wild generation ever since.

He's Still God

In this world, natural disasters will occur, terrorists will attack, accidents will happen, our financial status will change, good health will falter, children will get cancer, abuse will abound, and loved ones will die. Our knowledge of these truths causes us to dread the future, but there is no need to do so. God is already there. His goodness and mercy have gone ahead of us to secure our future. Whatever the outcome determined by humans or nature, God's plan alone will stand. "There are many plans in a man's heart, nevertheless, the LORD's counsel—that will stand" (Prov. 19:21 NKJV). And His plans can be trusted. Peace soothes our fears when we can say with the psalmist:

> When I am afraid,
> I will trust in you.
> In God, whose word I praise,
> in God I trust; I will not be afraid.
> What can mortal man do to me? (Ps. 56:3–4)

I was away speaking when a tornado struck the mid-South where my family and I live. My children were in lockdown at school for hours. My husband felt helpless as our daughter begged from her cell phone, "Come get me, Daddy. Please, hurry!" He was desperately trying to retrieve both of our children, but debris from the raging winds blocked his every path. Two hours later, he finally reached the school and found it, along with our children, untouched by the tornado. Our house had been passed over as well. Others were not as fortunate.

Driving home, I looked on in disbelief as I wove my way through the devastation. It felt as if my town had been ransacked by intruders. I felt cold and naked as I viewed the homes of friends and businesses that had been stripped bare. Then, I saw it. The church. "Not the church, Lord," I prayed as my heart sank. It had been a magnificent building standing tall and proud in our community. It had been the symbol of all that was good and right. Now it was wounded and exposed, stripped of beauty and glory. As destruction surrounded me, I looked to the heavens and questioned with great anxiety, "How will we survive this awful tragedy?"

Perhaps you are surrounded by trouble too. You're not alone, and you have nothing to fear. God is your support and your helper. You don't have to be perplexed, uncertain, or concerned about your future. You have no need to worry. God has promised to rescue you from every trial. "But I will rescue you on that day, declares the LORD; you will not be handed over to those you fear" (Jer. 39:17). Jesus promised that we would encounter trials in this fallen world. He said, "These things I have spoken to you, that in Me you may have peace. In the world you will have tribulation; but be of good cheer, I have overcome the world" (John 16:33 NKJV). We don't need to despair as long as our hope is in God. Hope helps us see the God of restoration instead of being paralyzed by the mess of destruction.

I'm thankful that we were not alone in our community. Volunteers, workmen, friends, and neighbors who put their hope in God worked together to rebuild our city. It was a precious sight, the evidence of hope and the reflection of love. Months later this truth became apparent as I drove by the church. The yard had been cleaned and the walls patched. It was still recovering from near destruction, but the message had not changed. Draped in a large sign that covered the front of the structure, the church declared to all, "HE'S STILL GOD!"

In this life will we ever be pressed and perplexed—yes, even crushed sometimes—but we never have to live in fear or despair (2 Cor. 4:8). No matter what storm we face, no matter what kind of trouble presses in or how bleak the unknown appears, the truth remains the same: "HE'S STILL GOD!"

The Worst Thing that Can Happen

When Porter died, a part of me died too. I thought nothing else could be worse than the pain and fear that surrounded me during those dark days. I ached inside. I felt so lost, empty, and alone. Anguish was my only friend. "If only Porter could come back long enough to see me through the pain, then I would be all right," I reasoned. "If he could just hold me once more, or if I could tell him all the things I wished I had told him while he was in the hospital, then his loss would be easier to bear," I assured myself.

At times, my need for his comforting touch was so strong it played tricks on my mind. Once, I saw a man with brown hair driving a red truck just like Porter's truck, and I followed him for miles. As my heart pounded with hope, nothing else mattered more in that moment than catching that truck. I was willing to drive to the ends of the earth if necessary. When I finally caught up with him at a red light and our eyes met, my fantasy came to a devastating halt. It felt as if the man in the truck had played a cruel joke on me. Weakened by the truth, I pulled over into a nearby parking lot, lay across the seat of my car, and wept for hours. Night began to fall as the sun set in the sky. I was chilled as the temperature inside the car turned cool. Sitting up, I wiped my face, zipped up my coat, and headed for home—without him.

Awful things may happen to us as a result of living in this fallen world, but our hope lies in God's everlasting and unchanging love. His love promises to sustain us, restore us, and make us new. It doesn't matter what we face in this life when we know that God, in His timing, *will* change the outcome, either in this world or the next. That's a promise! My hope is that one day I will be reunited with those I love who have gone on before me. Likewise, the disabled person will one day be made whole by the love of God. The lame will walk, and the blind will see. The deaf will hear, and the mute will speak, all by the power of love. "He will wipe every tear from their eyes. There will be no more death or mourning or crying or pain, for the old order of things has passed away" (Rev. 21:4).

While tragedy may touch our lives by way of sickness, a fallen economy, devastating wars, or the fury of a tsunami or tornado, the worst thing that can happen to a person is never to know the love of God and His saving grace. I came to this realization when I thought about the question Parker asked me, "What is the worst thing that can happen?"

Parker agreed, "Oh, yeah! If you don't know God's love, you can't be forgiven of your sins and go to heaven. Nothing is worse than that!"

Parker was right on target. Those without the love of God suffer not only in this world but also in the world to come. They will not be comforted or made whole. Instead, they will live separated from God forever. Can you imagine what it's like to be totally separated from God? The Bible calls it hell. This world in which we live is filled with much wickedness, immorality, and violence. Just think how much worse it would be without the presence of God caring for His own and holding back evil? Because of God's Spirit in the world, even those who do evil benefit from His mercy. Imagine what it would be like to live without that mercy forever.

Calamity, sickness, world hunger, debt, and death are not the worst things that can happen to a person. Even living in a Nazi concentration camp in World War II wasn't the worst of the worst. Corrie ten Boom and her sister, Betsie, spent years tormented as hostages of war in a concentration camp. Did they lose hope? No, because they put their hope in a sufficient, caring God who was bigger than their situation. Eventually both sisters were set free from their horrible bondage. Betsie found freedom in death as she entered into the presence of the Lord, but Corrie found freedom in the depths of God's love and spent the rest of her life proclaiming to all who would listen, "There is no pit so deep that He is not deeper still."[1]

Nothing we face on this earth is as tragic as not knowing the love of God. Once you and I are secure in His love, the Bible says nothing can separate us from Him. "Who shall separate us from the love of Christ? Shall tribulation, or distress, or persecution, or famine, or nakedness, or peril, or sword? … [N]or height nor depth, nor any other created thing, shall be able to separate us from the love of God which is in Christ Jesus our Lord" (Rom. 8:35, 39 NKJV). Holding our burdens before the cross, where God displayed His greatest love for you and me, allows us to know this: If you have Jesus, you have everything you need. Living without Him is the worst possible scenario for any man or woman.

Saved by a Boat

This world is full of pessimism. As Christians who live carefree in the care of God, we have no biblical right to wring our hands and wonder what we're going to do in the face of present-day troubles. Instead, Christ commanded that in the midst of persecution, confusion, wars, and rumors of wars, we are to encourage one another of His triumphant return when He'll put an end to it all (1 Thess. 4:18). On the other hand, millions of people in our world today have every reason to fear because their lives are so entangled with sin and selfishness. This describes not only our society, but the people of Noah's day, too. Yet in the midst of conflict, God has promised genuine peace, a sense of security that only He can provide. This kind of peace is not found in our world, nor is it found in trying to pacify our selfish desires. In Noah's day, the way of peace came by a boat.

When Noah finished the ark, God extended an invitation to him and his family to come aboard. The ark is a picture of salvation. In fact, we can see many similarities between Noah's ark and our salvation provided by Christ's death on the cross. Elmer L. Towns notes several parallels. The covering (roof) of the ark illustrates the atonement. Atonement means to cover one's sin. It's the process of establishing a right relationship with God. Christ is our atonement. His blood covers our sins and puts us back into right fellowship with God.

The size of the ark illustrates the sufficiency and greatness of Christ and His salvation: "And He Himself is the propitiation for our sins, and not for ours only but also for the whole world" (1 John 2:2 NKJV).

The ark had only one window at the top, and Noah had to look up to see out. This illustrates the place of prayer in the Christian's life: "My voice You shall hear in the morning, O LORD; in the morning I will direct it to You, and I will look up" (Ps. 5:3 NKJV).

Noah entered the ark through a single door. This points to Christ as the only way to God: "Jesus said to him, 'I am the way, the truth, and the life. No one comes to the Father except through Me'" (John 14:6 NKJV).

The ark illustrates the salvation experience of the believer. God's judgment was about to be unleashed on the world, but God provided a way of escape in the ark: "By faith Noah, being divinely warned of things not yet seen, moved with godly fear, prepared an ark for the saving of his household, by which he condemned the world and became heir of the righteousness which is according to faith" (Heb. 11:7 NKJV). All who fear God and His judgment are wise in receiving His salvation though Christ Jesus.

After Noah and his family entered the ark, the flood came. This illustrates baptism, which follows salvation. The flood didn't save Noah, his family, and the animals. The ark saved them. The flood washed away evil, cleansing the earth and making all things new. Likewise, baptism doesn't save the believer. Placing our trust in Christ's death and resurrection is our salvation. As a result, we are made new and clean, having been washed from our sin.[2]

It rained for forty days, but in the midst of destruction, God didn't forget Noah (Gen. 8:1). Eventually, the rain stopped and strong winds blew on the flood-soaked earth, evaporating the water and drying out the land. Noah, in partnership with God, entered the ark when God invited him to do so and waited there until he was told to leave. As a result, Noah and his family were spared from death.

Saved by a Cross

Some people don't know that life is a partnership with God. Because sin separates us from God, burdens weigh heavy on our souls. Until we learn to take Christ's yoke upon ourselves (Matt. 11:29), we'll never find peace. Therefore, anyone living apart from God can expect to be plagued by phobias, fears, and anxieties. Until people are reconciled to God, they are unpredictable and anxious creatures. Like Noah, their greatest need is a lifeboat.

I recall the first time Parker water-skied. He was having a great time while he was being pulled along by the boat. When he fell and let go of the rope, the connection to the boat was broken. Panic gripped his face as he watched the boat leave him behind. Drifting in unknown waters filled him with uncertainty. Anxious thoughts plagued his mind as he wondered whether his life jacket was trustworthy. It was only when the boat turned around and headed back in his direction that peace took hold again. When we pulled him back into the boat, he said with relief, "I didn't think anyone saw me fall. I thought you were gone for good." This is the kind of fright we live with when we are not connected to God. We know we can only tread water for so long on our own without the security of a boat.

The cross of Christ is our lifeboat that saves us from drowning in a sea of sin and selfishness. Christ's redemptive work on the cross has mended the partnership between God and us. Fearless living is achieved by making the choice to partner with God. Only then will our faith become stronger than all our fears. If you and I want to be rid of fear, we must stop putting our hope in the things of this world. We must "seek first the kingdom of God and His righteousness" (Matt. 6:33 NKJV) and learn to put the weight of our cares on Christ, who died for us.

Secondly, we need to refocus. Self-centeredness breeds anxiety. After I buried my husband, all I could think of was how I would survive and care for my son. I looked at my abilities and my bank account—both were inadequate. As long as my focus was on myself, I was paralyzed with fear. When I turned my focus from self to God, it made all the difference. My troubles looked small in comparison to my great God. In truth, worry and stress are really symptoms of self-sufficiency and a lack of trust in God.

Finally, we must commit ourselves wholly to God. Paul says, "All have sinned and fall short of the glory of God" (Rom. 3:23). That means that you and I have missed the mark. We can't get to God any other way except through His Son, Jesus. And "while we were still sinners, Christ died for us," bridging the gap between us and God (Rom. 5:8). Whoever wants Christ and believes He is who God says He is has been given the full benefit of being God's child (John 1:12).

The truly happy person is the one who has placed his trust in Christ alone for salvation. He has discovered that Christ's saving grace is the solution to sin, egotism, waywardness, and fears. You can see a profound difference in the person who chooses Christ as his lifeboat. Anxiety dissolves away like the mist in the morning sun. Peace rules the heart and mind. When troubles come, this person is able to live fearless in the presence of God.

If you are full of worry, then it may be that you have not fully given every area of your life to God. You can do so right now! All you have to do is acknowledge that you are a sinner and have been living a life separated from God, seeking your own will instead of His will. By using the following prayer as a guide, you can move beyond your sins and commit your life totally to God.

> Lord Jesus, I am a sinner. I believe You died for me and rose from the grave to purchase a place in heaven for me. Lord Jesus, come into my life and take control; forgive all my sins and save me. I'm placing my trust in You as I turn away from sin. Thank You, Jesus, for saving me, forgiving me, and filling me with peace. In Jesus' name I pray, amen.

If you sincerely asked God to forgive you, and you put your trust in Him alone, then you are secure in Christ's love. Nothing—no sin, no betrayal, no tragedy, no sickness, and not even death—can separate you from Him. However, I must warn you, if you have not decided to trust Christ, you are still making a choice. You're choosing to stand on your own. That choice, my friend, can have dire consequences.

Making the Right Choice

In an emergency, you only have a split second to make the right decision. You don't have time to think it over, list the pro and cons, or discuss it with a specialist. You have to make a choice and live with the result.

Hundreds of people in South Asia had only moments to make a life-saving decision when the horrifying tsunami of 2004 hit with its devastating rage. It was one of the deadliest natural disasters in history. I watched in sorrow on my television set as some had time to escape death while others, not so fortunate, were sent to a watery grave. As the death toll continued to rise, it was comforting to hear from those who survived. Each testimony reminded me of God's faithfulness in the midst of tragedy. One man's story stuck in my mind. I listened intently as he told of his escape.

He shared how the people scattered like frantic mice, running in every direction, when the giant wave attacked. Most of the people took the broad road, pushing and shoving one another, as they tried to escape. It appeared to be the logical choice to this man as well. Just when he was about to join them, he noticed a man running in the opposite direction from the crowd. He was a native. Something inside the interviewee told him to follow the native. Instantly, he called to his family, and they escaped by the narrow road. With only a moment to decide, he chose to follow the road less traveled. By taking the narrow path, he and his entire family were saved.

As in this man's testimony, the Bible speaks of two different roads. Whether we are conscious of it or not, each of us chooses the road we will travel in life. We follow either the broad way or the narrow way. The wide road seems the more favorable. It's considered Easy Street. You'll have an abundance of company on this road, because it's familiar, comfortable, and appears to be the most logical way. Unfortunately, it "leads to destruction" (Matt. 7:13). The other road is narrow, difficult, and sometimes lonely. Taking the narrow road is the first step toward total dependence on God, and it leads to life, both now and forever. If you look carefully, you can see a man, God's Son, standing on the narrow path faithfully calling, "Follow Me." He says, "I am the way and the truth and the life. No one comes to the Father except through me" (John 14:6).

Today, as the wave of sin, rebellion, and fear attempts to drown you, the Lord is providing a way of escape. Two roads lie before you. Time is short, so you need to make a decision—now. As long as you stay on the wide road, destruction will follow. Choosing the narrow path leads to life. Today is the day. Now is the time. Which path will you choose—life or death?

Concerning our future, Paul promises, "For the Lord Himself will descend from heaven with a shout, with the voice of an archangel, and with the trumpet of God. And the dead in Christ will rise first. Then we who are alive and remain shall be caught up together with them in the clouds to meet the Lord in the air. And thus we shall always be with the Lord" (1 Thess. 4:16–17 NKJV). Someday in heaven, our fears will be no more, and our faith will be perfected. Earth will be but a distant memory as we live in the glorious presence of our King.

C. S. Lewis puts it this way: "As organs in the Body of Christ, as stones and pillars in the temple, we are assured of our eternal self-identity and shall live to remember the galaxies as an old tale."[3] You and I can live carefree in the loving care of Christ when we allow Him to deliver us from the perils of present trouble by securing our future in Him and making heaven our eternal home.

Christ's provision goes far beyond heaven and earth. When you and I face the unknown, God is there, leading the way through our unknown territory until we are safe on the other side.

Bible Study: Know It—Stow It—Show It

With all the news stations and talk radio, it's hard to determine what's really going on in our world today. Does anyone know the truth? Yes—the Spirit of God knows. While reports of current events can cause great alarm, we can find peace by seeking God's perspective on wars, earthquakes, and international conflict. His Word counsels us about how to face changing worldviews in our marriages, workplace, and parent-child relationships without being filled with terror.

1. In Mark 13, we find God's perspective. Jesus is telling His disciples how to prepare for and recognize the times in which they live. Read verses 5–8 and list the signs Jesus describes.

2. In verse 9, what counsel does Jesus give?

3. Jesus tells us in verse 11 that we have no need to be anxious about these things. Why not?

4. What does Proverbs 3:5 warn us against?

5. We're to walk by faith and rely on the Holy Spirit to show us what to do when we need to know what to do. When you're

faced with a situation or an unexpected tragedy, you can rely on the Holy Spirit to guide you, to even give you what to say. How does this help you to release your fears and grow in confidence?

6. List some situations where you need to rely on the Holy Spirit for direction.

7. What does Mark 13:13 say about believers going through hard times?

8. Scripture says that the one who endures—which means to stand firm to the end—will be saved. What does it mean to stand firm until the end?

9. Are we saved by enduring hard times, pulling ourselves up by our bootstraps, and living to the best of our ability? Is endurance proof of our salvation? Explain, and then compare your answer to Jude 24.

10. True or false: Endurance is an outward sign of the genuineness of your profession of faith in Christ.

11. Give an example from your own life of endurance that expressed genuine faith.

12. In your present situation, how would it benefit you to stand firm and allow the Holy Spirit to show you what to do to combat fear?

Like the disciples, you and I need to seek Christ during days of trouble. We do that by knowing His Word. "Your word is a lamp to my feet and a light for my path" (Ps. 119:105). In times of trouble, whether it's in our family, workplace, community, church, or world, we have to get understanding from the Holy Spirit, who leads us in all truth and supplies supernatural strength to endure until the end by faith, not fear.

Chapter Eight
Overcoming the Fear of the Unknown

Knowing the love of Christ and securing our future in Him doesn't guarantee that we won't face uncertainties. What we can be certain of is God's provision as He guides us through unknown lands.

In the middle of the night, my husband and I were awakened by the telephone. Alarmed, I listened intently to my husband's conversation to determine who was calling. It was our twenty-one-year-old son. He had fallen asleep at the wheel while driving home from a friend's house. This was his second wreck in three years. He'd escaped the first crash unharmed, but I felt terror as I waited to hear if he'd been so fortunate this time. He assured his dad that he was okay, but the car was totaled. "Just look for the flashing lights of the emergency vehicles on the interstate heading north, and you'll know where I am," Mitch said, still shaken by the accident.

Mitch was only four months old when his biological father died. Since he was four years old, Pat had been the only dad he had ever known. Pat left immediately after receiving Mitch's call, leaving me behind with our two other children, who were still sleeping. I waited alone with no one to keep me company but my worry.

When Pat arrived, he found Mitch's demolished car hugging the mangled fifty-foot guardrail that had kept him from crossing the highway into oncoming traffic. Mitch, however, had not suffered a single scratch, bruise, or broken bone—not one. His dad was stunned, but the policeman was even more astonished. According to my husband, the officer shared words of wisdom with Mitch, "I'm proud of you, son, for being clean, but you still shouldn't be out this late at night. And if I were you, I wouldn't go home and go to bed. I'd go to the nearest church and thank God for saving your life, because He obviously has a purpose for it. I've seen many wrecks just like yours, but I've never seen anyone walk away from a scene like this one. Your mom and dad should be standing in the funeral home today looking over your dead body. Instead, a guardrail stopped your car from crossing into oncoming traffic—the only guardrail in miles of this highway. You stepped out of a mangled car in one piece as if nothing happened. That's a miracle if I've ever seen one!" It was as if God was speaking through the officer. Pat drove Mitch home in silence. The policeman had said it all. What more could he add?

Later that morning, we were met with even sadder news. One of our church youths, a sixteen-year-old boy, was not so lucky that same Saturday night. Depressed and distraught, he had taken a gun to his head and killed himself. A part of me was thankful that God had spared Mitch's life. We had come to church to praise Him for that. The other part of me was brokenhearted for this mother who lost her son. Terrified of what might have been, I grieved for both myself and this devastated mother. *I could have been her,* I thought fearfully. For twenty-one years, I'd allowed the possibility of my son's death to torment me. My mother-in-law lost her son at a young age.

It could happen to me, too, right? Now my nightmare was too close for comfort. He had escaped this time, but my concerns were still not laid to rest.

Sunday afternoon, Pat and I drove Mitch to the junkyard to retrieve Mitch's personal belongings from the car. Pat pulled up in front of the damaged car. He and Mitch went into the office to present the registration form that allowed us to enter the car. It was then, sitting there alone, that I noticed the date 9-9 painted in large orange numbers across the windshield of the mangled car. That's when it hit me. Mitch's accident had occurred on the anniversary of his father's death. Stranger still, they were exactly the same age. My worst fear was staring me in the face. All of a sudden, as my eyes fixed on the date, I realized it was a message from God—an undeniable, clear sign from above. Mitch was in the hands of God. "That's right," I said to myself. "He is. Therefore, Satan, you can't scare me anymore."

God has a different plan for Mitch than He had for his dad. I always knew that truth intellectually, but that day in the junkyard, it became a reality. How could I doubt God anymore when my son walked away from a near-death experience on the anniversary of his father's death? I couldn't. Not only did this experience prove that God is in control, but it confirmed that I was not. The only power I have as a parent is to get on my knees and relinquish all my fears to God while trusting in His good and perfect plan for my children. The only power you and I have over any fear is to place it in God's care.

Usually our concerns never come to pass anyway. The plane doesn't crash, you don't lose your job, your child doesn't choose the wrong crowd, you don't fail to wake up in morning, you don't stop

fitting in, and you don't cease to succeed. Even if our greatest worries do come true, we must not allow ourselves to be taunted day
and night by "What if?" We must trust God's plan. Regardless of our
spooks, God's plan alone stands firm and true. Despite the outcome,
we can rest in His perfect purpose for our lives, relying on this truth:
"'For I know the plans I have for you,' declares the LORD, 'plans
to prosper you and not to harm you, plans to give you hope and a
future'" (Jer. 29:11).

Worrying Doesn't Change the Future

The fear of the unknown is not only nerve-racking; it can also cause
us to live on pins and needles as we spend precious energy anticipating the worst-case scenario. Pastor and Bible teacher David Jeremiah
offers us a biblical definition of worry:

> The New Testament word for *worry* is translated by the
> phrase "to take thought" or "to be careful." It comes
> from the Greek word which means to have a divided
> mind. So, to be a worrier is to have your mind divided
> between legitimate thoughts and thoughts that are
> not legitimate—thoughts which you shouldn't be
> thinking.
>
> Worry is future-focused. The person who worries has
> two problems: The future is not here, and the future is
> not his.[1]

The future is unknown. We can't control it. That's why Jesus says
three times in Matthew 6:25–34, "Do not worry." When you and I

are tempted to worry, we should heed Christ's advice and not do it. Worrying won't change the outcome. It only steals our peace.

A lack of worry about the unknown future doesn't mean we are unconcerned or don't plan ahead. Carefree living is not the same as careless living. Still, while the future may be out of our hands, it's not out of the hands of an adequate and trustworthy God. When we face a worrisome, unknown situation, we can look to Joshua as an example.

Follow the Leader

It's recorded in the first chapter of Joshua that after Moses died, God passed the baton of leadership to Joshua. The Israelites had been wandering in the desert for forty years under the guidance of Moses. Now, under a new leader, their journey was almost over. Just beyond the Jordan River was their Promised Land—the land that God had guaranteed to Abraham and his descendants.

Upon reaching the Jordan River, Joshua and the Israelites set up camp by the stream and awaited God's direction. As when they faced the Red Sea, God was going to have to make a way for them to cross the river. On the third day, God told the officers to instruct the people that when they saw the ark of the covenant, they should follow it, because they had "never been this way before" (Josh. 3:4).

You see, friend, God understands our fear of the unknown. He realizes that you may be in a situation you've never passed through before and that you're afraid. It may be the first time you've been without employment. Maybe you've just been diagnosed with an illness or your child is in rebellion. You've never been down this road before, and you don't know which way to go or what to do. God will guide the way.

The ark carried God's presence, and only the priests were to carry it. "And as soon as the priests who carry the ark of the LORD—the Lord of all the earth—set foot in the Jordan, its waters flowing downstream will be cut off and stand up in a heap" (Josh. 3:13). The people were instructed on how closely they should follow the ark. Without this instruction, the people would have crowded the ark, and God wanted every person to be able to see His presence faithfully leading them through the unknown valley. What greater encouragement could they have than this—that the Lord was their God, a God who was with them?

The same is true for us today. Just as God guided the Israelites through unknown territory, He will guide you and me, too. When we come to a place we've never passed through before, God is always present to help us. As He said through Isaiah,

> When you pass through the waters, I will be with you;
> And through the rivers, they shall not overflow you.
> When you walk through the fire, you shall not be burned,
> Nor shall the flame scorch you.
> For I am the LORD your God,
> The Holy One of Israel, your Savior. (Isa. 43:2–3 NKJV)

I hope you're beginning to see that living in the awareness of God's unseen presence and trusting completely in His providential care is the antidote to fear.

Joshua's life was unpredictable and full of unknowns, much like yours and mine. Yet, he endured, as Moses did, seeing Him who is unseen (Heb. 11:27). The Greek root word for *endurance* alludes to the capacity to bear up under difficulty. It takes endurance not to give way to fear but to press forward with our eyes firmly fixed on our leader—Jesus Christ. Joshua successfully resisted fear by keeping his focus on God rather than the events surrounding him. Like the Israelites, we are sometimes called to move forward without detailed instructions. Even though the children of Israel were not told how they would pass over the river, the people went forth in faith. We too can move forward in faith, sharing in the promised presence of God leading the way through our unknown circumstances.

Finding Peace in the Unknown

This was true for Annie. It started out like any other evening at home. Annie had an aerobics class after work, so Donny prepared dinner. It was a good arrangement. Donny had a beautiful, slim wife, and Annie didn't have to cook. Dinner was put on hold until she got home, because that's when the family enjoyed sharing about their day. But on this night, their lives were about to unexpectedly change forever. In the middle of dinner, Annie's right hand suddenly went numb. Unable to hold her fork, she dropped it to the floor.

"Are you okay?" Donny asked. Annie felt ill, and her head was pounding. It was the kind of pain that made you know that something was wrong.

The next day, Annie told her doctor about the numbness, the nausea, and the severe pain in her head. After viewing the MRI of her head, the doctor informed Annie that her condition was beyond his expertise and he was sending her to see the best neurologist in the country. Terror of the unknown crept into Annie's heart, causing her to break out in a cold sweat. Her heart pounded within her sweaty chest as a lump that she couldn't swallow formed in her throat. Annie was petrified.

When she and her husband arrived at the neurologist's office, the waiting room was crowded. Annie's anxieties heightened when they bypassed the waiting room and were taken straight back to see the doctor. He informed Annie that he had bad news and good news. The bad news was Annie had a brain aneurysm. The good news was it was operable. Alarmed by the dreadful news, Annie fell to pieces as the doctor explained the procedure. He would start by shaving her head where the incision would be made. Then, the brain specialist would remove the left part of Annie's skull. He carefully explained that he would have to stop her heart for a split second and put a metal clamp around the artery in her brain. This would definitely affect her speech for a while. The doctor couldn't guarantee how things would turn out, but he was hopeful. Distressed, both Annie and Donny melted with grief.

After sharing the news with friends and family, Annie sank into deep depression. The unknowns of her condition left her scared stiff. Her mind raced with possible outcomes. She didn't want to see or talk to anyone. She didn't get out of bed or bathe for days, until she decided to visit her priest and receive the sacrament for the sick. Annie believed this sacrament was for those who were dying. She felt that after receiving it and praying with the priest, she would have the peace she needed to face death. Peace didn't come.

"I need something more," Annie confessed to the priest.

"That is what you need," the priest said as he pointed to the large crucifix hanging at the front of the church. Annie walked slowly toward the cross, knelt down in front of it, and cried out to her Lord.

"If it's time for my life to come to an end, I'm willing to surrender to your will. Just give me strength to make it." At the exact moment that Annie placed her life before God, she felt a warm breeze come over like a ray of sunshine falling across her face. Her whole being was filled with peace. She had no more tears. Somehow Annie knew that no matter what—live or die—everything was going to be fine.

Annie's surgery was a success. It took several months before she could speak again, but Annie didn't mind. She was at peace. Annie was more than at peace; she was thankful. Her aneurysm brought her to a dividing place in her life. She could either continue the way she had always lived, or she could depend on God. She chose the latter, and it changed her life for good.

Something amazing happens when we faithfully cry out to the Lord, believing in His perfect care. Our faith suddenly becomes stronger than our fear. Let me tell you a little secret: None of us knows how to act or what to do during a crisis. However, if we will fall on our face before His throne in total weakness and cry out, He will strengthen and lead us. This is God's promise. Paul writes that God told him, "My grace is sufficient for you, for my power is made perfect in weakness" (2 Cor. 12:9). So go ahead and be weak when the crisis comes—just remember to run to the One who is your strength and lay all your cares at His feet.

Surrendered Fears Pave the Road for Fearless Living

Yes, something miraculous happens when we yield our lives to Christ. Surrender is not just a one-time action we take when we first give ourselves to Christ. Yielding our will to God's will is a day-by-day, moment-by-moment, even minute-by-minute way of life for the believer. Surrender is challenging, but it wasn't meant to be that way. It's where fearless living begins.

Have you ever considered why God asks us to surrender our will to His will? It's because once Jesus has full reign over our lives, then we have all that He is! We have His wisdom, His faith, His power, and His holiness. It's almost too wonderful! It's the very life you and I are struggling to obtain in our own power every day—and can't. The reason we can't is because God doesn't just improve us like a remodeled house. No, He exchanges His life and His nature for ours. In order for us to experience His life in ours, we have to make a choice. We can either continue to live our lives our own way—by holding on to fear, doubt, and control—or we can die to self and allow Jesus to live His life of wisdom, faith, power, and holiness through us.

Jesus said, "Whoever finds his life will lose it, and whoever loses his life for my sake will find it" (Matt. 10:39). What Christ is saying is that you and I can keep our life the way it is right now, but we'll just end up losing it. Or, we can give it completely to Him and find life on a whole new level. It's only by choosing Jesus and abandoning self that we can experience His presence and power in our lives. The reason surrender is the way to go is it allows us to follow His plan for our lives, which is so much better than our own plan. Yielding to God's will means that when we come face-to-face with a problem we've never encountered before, we can maintain our peace and actually look forward to the next step God has for us.

I heard a story about a professional football player who was an all-star player until the day he broke his leg. The doctor told him the break was so bad he would never play football again. With sympathy, each of his teammates expressed to him how sorry they were for his misfortune. To everyone's surprise, the athlete expressed great joy and excitement instead of sorrow and concern about his future. That's because he was a surrendered child of God. When the football player was asked why he wasn't saddened by the accident, he explained that since God allowed his football career to come to an end, a new adventure must be awaiting him, and he couldn't wait to find out where God was leading. He was willing to press through his fear and look ahead to a new adventure with God. In order to move ahead, he had to leave behind the old to gain the new.

Is God trying to move you off your old land onto new land? If so, He can be trusted with your unknown future. Remember, it's not unknown to Him. He has a plan far beyond our suffering. He will not let our trials go to waste. No, God will use them for our good and His glory—if we allow Him.

The need to control our circumstances is not God's plan for you and me. His plan involves a lifestyle change that embraces trust as we relinquish control in favor of doing His will. We don't have to struggle to live *for* God. We simply have to let go and allow God to live His life *through* us. The apostle Paul puts it this way: "I have been crucified with Christ and I no longer live, but Christ lives in me. The life I live in the body, I live by faith in the Son of God, who loved me and gave himself for me" (Gal. 2:20). Surrendering our will for God's changes the way we live. It also quiets our anxieties as we wait for God's next assignment.

Taking Every Thought Captive

What we think determines what we believe, and what we believe determines how we live. The football player's thoughts and beliefs led him to live a yielded life of trust and expectancy, while Annie's thoughts convinced her she was doomed. Believing she was going to die affected how she lived. Annie's fear turned to depression. She wouldn't eat, bathe, or seek the comfort and help of her family and friends. Fearful thoughts of the unknown can make us physically, emotionally, and spiritually sick. But fearless living is achieved when we take captive every thought that doesn't line up with God's truths.

Paul says that "we demolish arguments and every pretension that sets itself up against the knowledge of God, and we take captive every thought to make it obedient to Christ" (2 Cor. 10:5). Either our thoughts can take us captive, or we can take them captive. The difference lies in where we place our focus. If we focus on our circumstances, they will seem like undefeatable giants. If our focus is on God, we'll recognize that He is greater than our present situation.

What fearful thoughts have gripped you concerning your situation? Ask yourself, "Do I trust in what I can see or imagine, or do I trust in who I know?" David trusted in God.

God spent years preparing David to be king of Israel. Along the way, David developed a close, personal relationship with God, a relationship built on faith. The day David faced the Philistine giant, Goliath, every principle God had taught him came together in one defining moment. First Samuel 17 records the historical event.

All the soldiers of Israel were too frightened to face the taunting giant. They believed what they could see with their eyes instead of trusting in the unseen hand of God. Not David. His confidence was in the Lord even though he might have been shaking in his sandals. David didn't allow thoughts of fear and defeat to paralyze him.

Instead, he took his thoughts captive and recalled the truth about the God who had led him in past victories. He later said:

> My God is my rock, in whom I take refuge,
> my shield and the horn of my salvation.
> He is my stronghold, my refuge and my savior—
> from violent men you save me. (2 Sam. 22:3)

God was not just David's shield. He shields all who take refuge in Him (verse 31).

Instead of allowing his mind to worry, David took refuge in the Lord by remembering God's faithfulness in the past. This enabled him to trust God in his present situation. David was convinced that the battle belonged to the Lord, and God would come to his rescue and conquer the enemy just as He had in the past. The same is true for us. When we trust God in a crisis situation, no matter how big or frightening it may be, it always leads to a greater confidence in God for the future.

With God on his side, David gathered five smooth stones and stepped onto the battlefield to face the giant. To those watching, Goliath's victory seemed certain, but David had the favor of God. When God's on your team, you're on the winning side. Fixing his eyes on the giant, David swallowed his terror as he reached for the leather satchel that hung around his hips. Removing one stone, he placed it in his slingshot and sent it whirling at the giant's head. Goliath went down and never got up again, proving once more God's faithfulness. David was victorious in this battle because he knew his Lord. David knew He was the God of Israel, the Lord of Hosts, and able to win the battle. In order to take captive the lies of the Enemy, you and I must know our God.

David also relied on God's supernatural strength for the task. No one had the ability to fight the giant. While the army of Israel focused on defeat, David focused on God's provision. The army trusted in themselves, but David trusted in God. He was successful because he believed God was able to conquer the giant even though he was afraid.

Like David, you and I must learn to take our worrisome thoughts captive. Right thinking leads to right living. Imagine that your thoughts of doubt and fear are floating around in the air. Symbolically grab hold of one and say, "Lord, take captive this thought and hold it obedient to You, Jesus Christ." Amazingly, in this act we find the power to change our thinking. As we practice taking each stray thought captive, our thoughts begin to reflect the mind of Christ, and so do our actions.

For years, I lived in anxiety, watching my children's every move, trying to determine what they were going to do next. My fears of the unknown led me to imagine all sorts of things that could bring them harm. These worried thoughts led to fear-driven parenting. Fear not only suffocated me, but it caused me to smother my children. My phobias tarnished my relationships, my faith, and my prayer life. Taking my thoughts captive has changed what I believe. Instead of waiting for the phone to ring in the middle of the night, I sleep soundly. I no longer worry about my children's future or if they will go down the wrong road. I've stopped questioning their interests that don't line up with mine. Instead, I've become their biggest fan, supporting them in all their endeavors. Strangely, closing the door on my fears has opened up a whole new relationship with each of them. They share more with me than they ever did before. In turn, this allows me to be a continued influence in my children's lives—not out of fear, but out of love. Taking our thoughts of fear and doubt captive is putting to death a tarnished piece of ourselves and replacing it with a polished attribute of Christ.

You Have to Die to Live

Even as we grow in our faith, unpleasant things will still happen to us in this world. They're out of our control. Yet in God's economy, every fear, every pain, every sorrow, and every loss is not wasted. God uses these little deaths to make us more like Him. Anne Graham Lotz says it best: "God has used pressures and pain and problems in my life as the nails that have pinned me to the cross. By submitting to Him in those things, I have entered into an experience of death to myself."[2] I can identify with that. Can you? Some of the nails in my life have been the death of my husband, pains of childhood, disappointments, watching my sister and brother-in-law suffer when he lost his job, overcoming fear, surrendering to ministry, getting on a plane and leaving my family several times a year for speaking engagements, the betrayal of friends, concerns for my children's well-being, ministering to a lifelong friend with breast cancer, watching addiction enslave my brother, and not being able to help my wayward nephew. What are some of your nails?

Each small death has brought me closer to God and His life plan for me. And guess what? His plan is better than I ever imagined or could have created on my own. In order for you and me to change from fearful living to fearless living, we must be willing to surrender our fears of the unknown, take our thoughts captive, and keep our eyes on our Leader. Even if you're in a place that you've never passed through before, you have the assurance of God's guidance.

How valuable to you is the presence of God and His supernatural strength when you're facing the unknown? The amazing truth is, you don't have to wait until you or your loved one has a crisis that leaves you weak and afraid of the unknown. You can surrender your anxious thoughts about the future now. When trouble comes, and it's always going to come while we live in this fallen world, you will be prepared to exercise faith in God's perfect care. Even though chaos may be going on around you, you'll be living above it—soaring on the wings of the Most High God, who knows the way through new, uncharted territory.

"Yes, yes!" you say. This is the reason you came to Christ in the first place—to live above the chaos in the world, to conquer sin, and to secure your place in heaven. Yet sometimes you and I fail. Perhaps this causes you to live in fear of God's punishment, because you didn't live up to His standards. God doesn't want us to be afraid of Him but to love Him. It's only when you and I respect God's name, power, and ways that we come to understand His love, which, in turn, eliminates our fear.

Bible Study: Know It—Stow It—Show It

People like David are not necessarily brave people. They're just as weak, afraid, and needy as everyone else. The difference is that they've come to accept their weaknesses and rely on God's strength rather than their own. They are intentional about trusting God and surrendering all their fears to His faithful care. That makes all the difference.

1. For fifteen years, David had been running for his life from King Saul. God had told him that he would be the next king, but his life showed no evidence that God was going to fulfill His promise. It looked just the opposite, like David was going to lose his life before he got to the throne. Read 1 Samuel 30:1–5. Why did David and his people weep until they could weep no more?

2. a. Have you ever been so devastated by fear that you wept until you couldn't cry anymore? If so, describe that time.

   b. Did you ever run from fear? For how long?

   c. Where and when did you find comfort?

3. Read 1 Samuel 30:6 and record what David did when the people wanted to kill him.

4. Where do you go to find strength and encouragement when you're afraid?

A parent

A friend

A pastor

God

Other (name where)

When everything seemed against David, he turned to the Lord for inner peace and strength.

5. In 1 Samuel 30:8, we see that David did something else in his time of terror and discouragement. What did he do?

6. Write out these verses: Exodus 13:21, 15:13; Psalm 32:8, 48:14; John 16:13. What do all these verses have in common?

When you're so afraid that things seem hopeless, and you feel helpless not knowing what to do, turn to God for direction. Not only will He strengthen you, but He also promises to guide you and show you the way to victory.

7. We don't have to be Lone Ranger Christians when we are filled with anxieties. Look at 1 Samuel 30:7–8. Who does David ask for help? What kind of help does he seek?

You and I can ask the help of a godly friend, mentor, or pastor to help us overcome our worries. David asked the priest to bring him the ephod. This was a pouch that housed two stones known as the Urim and the Thummim. They helped the people determine God's will. Today, you and I have God's Word to guide us into all truth and communicate His will for our lives. Between the pages of His Word, we find God's truth so we can recognize Satan's lies and take those thoughts captive.

8. As people of God, we should be people of joy, peace, and faith in any situation, known or unknown. Yet many are battling worry daily. How can you use what you learned in this chapter to help you achieve a life of faith instead of fear?

Chapter Nine
The Right Kind of Fear

When I first married Pat, I was gung ho about being a good wife. I had great intentions of cooking, cleaning, and supporting my husband as a godly wife ought to do. I was off to a good start. The first four days of our marriage, I got up, brushed my hair and teeth, put on my silky new bridal housecoat, and made his breakfast. As he ate, I sat across the table from him and sipped my coffee with a smile. Up to this point, I'm sure he thought he had married well.

Then day five came, and without warning, my allergy to mornings returned. It couldn't be helped. I had to break the news to Pat: "Well, I did my best, but it's over. You're on your own, pal." Back to bed I went. Did this mean that I didn't love him anymore? No. Could Pat have interpreted my actions that way? Yes. Most people equate love with respect. When a man has the love and respect of his wife, it affects his whole well-being. He feels as if he can conquer the world. I'm thankful for discovering this truth. While I'm not perfect, I've learned to show Pat as often as I can the love and admiration I have for him and that he's worthy to receive it.

Respect is not only valuable in marriage—it's significant in all relationships. What would our world look like if spouses respected one another, children honored their parents, citizens obeyed the laws and authorities, and all people revered the Lord? What if we had a type of wise fear that motivated us to do right and respect others? Our world would look the way God intended it to look.

Not all fear is bad. In some cases, knowledge begins with a healthy fear (Prov. 1:7). It can motivate us to do right, respect others, and obey both secular and religious laws. In fact, from Genesis to Revelation we are commanded to obey God's laws through love and respect for Him and others.

The right kind of fear motivates us to obey God, respect our spouses, honor our parents, and live by the rules of society meant to protect us from danger, sinning, and the consequences that come from bad choices. Those who respect God are motivated to walk in obedience. God gives life, security, and blessings to those who revere Him and walk in obedience to His ways. He shows them compassion, fulfills their desires, and gives them peace.

Obedience Brings Freedom

If we were to survey the level of respect we have for one another today, we'd find many have lost respect not only for God's authority but for those in the majority of other relationships as well. While everybody wants to be loved, few are disciplined enough to be under the authority of another. It's a free world, right? Why shouldn't we live as such?

It was our desire for self-government that brought fear into our lives from the start, way back in the garden of Eden. But we were not created to live apart from God. The Lord is calling you and me to a relationship where love, honor, and obedience are the foundation on which all else is built—because "happy are those who fear the Lord" (Ps. 112:1, paraphrased).

To have godly fear means to revere and hold God in awe, not offending Him with sin. This is a good kind of fear. Reverential fear is a noble and healthy fear of God's greatness and holiness. It's a type of fear that respects the Lord and His ways much like the fear that alerts us to respect danger. For example, I have a fear of snakes, vicious dogs, and high places. When I encounter these harmful situations, fear is working for my good. When I see a snake, fear warns me to flee and avoid a painful or poisonous bite. If I encounter a vicious dog, fear warns me to stay away and avoid attack. Fear of high places prevents me from moving close to the edge where I could fall over.

I also have a healthy fear that motivates me to respect my marriage. I wouldn't do anything to hurt my relationship with my husband for fear of the results. Not only would it hurt my husband and children deeply if I were to have an affair, but it would also affect my marriage on all levels. Likewise, Pat, who works in an office full of women, shows me respect by obeying my wishes. He doesn't go to lunch alone with a woman or put himself in any other position where he is alone with a female coworker. The fear of consequences keeps both Pat and me from stepping across the boundaries of our marriage commitment. Knowing that we are both committed to our promise brings peace of mind instead of worry. It creates carefree living. As long as healthy fear motivates me to obey my marriage commitment, I don't have to worry about having an affair. In other words, obedience brings freedom to my life. This is exactly the way godly fear works. Real danger produces the fear of consequences, so we choose to obey and avoid those consequences, and this obedience results in carefree living. In other words, the right kind of fear works for us instead of against us.

One of my favorite stories of the Bible is recorded in Genesis 22. At God's command, Abraham was about to take his son's life even though God had promised to make a great nation through Abraham's son Isaac. While it didn't make sense for God to ask for Isaac's life, Abraham trusted God. You see, God doesn't always explain His reasons for asking us to do the hard stuff in life. He does, however, expect our obedience, and obedience comes naturally when we love, revere, and trust our heavenly Father.

Abraham was able to count on God because he had a history with the Lord. Time and again God had proved Himself faithful in Abraham's life. While Abraham didn't know how God would do it, he believed God would either spare Isaac or bring him back to life. Those were the only ways to fulfill God's promise to build a great nation through Isaac. As Abraham was about to kill his own son, an angel of the Lord stopped him. "Abraham, Abraham! … Do not lay a hand on the lad, or do anything to him; for now I know that you fear God, since you have not withheld your son, your only son, from Me" (Gen. 22:11–12 NKJV). What an amazing moment in the relationship between Abraham and God. Abraham was obedient, and God was faithful.

Whenever I read about this event, I can almost picture the scene in my mind. I envision Abraham standing over his son, distraught and in anguish as sweat pours from his brow. For a moment he turns away to gain composure, then clenches his teeth and lifts the knife high into the air, pausing just long enough to secure control of his quivering hand. Suddenly, he hears a voice from heaven, "Abraham, don't touch him!" Instantly, tension melts into relief as he drops the knife and bursts into tears of joy. I can almost hear the cling of the knife's blade as it falls against rocks on its way to the ground. Abraham scoops his boy up into his arms and kisses his face repeatedly. Under his breath, he praises the Lord—"Thank You, God. Thank You."

God never wanted Isaac dead. His desire was Abraham's surrendered heart. A yielded heart is a reverent heart and one that God blesses. "He will bless those who fear the LORD—small and great alike" (Ps. 115:13). Other benefits of fearing God are:

> The fear of the LORD leads to life:
> Then one rests content, untouched by trouble. (Prov. 19:23)

> He fulfills the desires of those who fear him;
> he hears their cry and saves them. (Ps. 145:19)

> His mercy extends to those who fear him,
> from generation to generation. (Luke 1:50)

Yet we shouldn't fear the Lord just for the benefits we receive. It's our reasonable service to show admiration to our God who showers us with goodness. This principle is true in our relationships with others, too. Honor and respect go hand in hand, as we see in the relationship between Abraham and Isaac.

Commentators estimate Isaac's age to be much older than a boy. He was probably a young man in his late teens or early twenties. Certainly a boy of this age could have stopped his aging father, who insisted on tying him to an altar. Since Isaac didn't fight back, we can assume that he obediently complied with his father's wishes. Isaac revealed a healthy fear of his father. He trusted that his father knew best. Isaac's actions were proof that he had been raised to love, honor, and respect his father without question.

Unfortunately, we've lost this type of fear in our society today. With less and less respect for authority, children rebel against parents, marriages suffer infidelity, laws are broken, and the grace of God is taken for granted.

No Respect

When I was pregnant with my third child, I shamefully displayed a lack of respect for a police officer. It was a Wednesday afternoon, and I was running late for church. On the way, I had to drop off my eldest son at baseball practice. The fact that he had practice on a church night, not to mention in the drizzling rain, already had my tail feathers up in the air. I was in no mood to get my second child out of the car in the rain to walk my baseball player down to the playing field, nor did I have the time. When we are short on time, what do we do? You guessed it. I sped right into the park, where the policeman pulled me over.

I was appalled! How could he set up a speed trap in the park on a rainy day to catch a pregnant woman who was running late for church! "The nerve!" I thought. By now, I'd had it. Before the officer could approach my car, I jumped out in the rain and met him halfway. "Are you going to give me a ticket?" I questioned with one hand on my hip and the other pointing in his face. He didn't speak, nor did his expression change, so I continued. "I thought it was outrageous enough that these boys have to practice ball on a church night in the rain, but *nooooo!* Being set up for a speed trap in the park takes the cake!"

"Ma'am, I'm sorry," he apologized.

"Well, you should be," I whispered under my breath.

"I can't do anything about your son's practice, but I can assure you I can do something about your speeding," he said, firmly pulling his ticket pad from his coat pocket. "Furthermore," he added, "if you continue to disrespect my authority, I can do something about that, too."

Disrespect his authority? Is that what I did? Unfortunately, it was exactly what happened. While I'd like to blame my behavior on my hormones, I can't. I was guilty on all accounts. As I cowered back to my car, I noticed my children's faces pressed against the backseat window. They were no doubt learning how to disrespect authority—from their mother.

I let what I thought were my rights blind me to truth. It was my duty to submit to the police officer's authority. Regrettably, this kind of behavior goes on every day in the workplace, the home, and even in the church. Can you imagine what our world would look like today if respect ruled? We would have a feeling of security, with gestures of love freely given and received. Common courtesies would be raised from the dead. We'd make an effort to know our neighbors and lend a helping hand to a stranger. The words *fear* and *anxiety* would be dropped from the language. Peace and goodwill would be the heartbeat of our existence. That world begins with people having a healthy dose of godly fear.

God the Father

What does it mean when God reveals himself to us as Father and adopts us into His forever family through faith in Jesus Christ? It means you and I should have a childlike reverence for His age, wisdom, power, and authority. We can look to Him as the source for all our needs and feel secure in His love. We honor Him as Father by exhibiting the same godly fear that Abraham and Isaac revealed.

Today the emphasis on honoring fathers is much different than in Isaac's day or even a hundred years ago. No longer do we acknowledge the command, "Honor your father and your mother" (Ex. 20:12), which also applies to the relationship we have with our heavenly Father. Rodney Dangerfield is not the only person who suffers from "no respect." These days our society has a general lack of respect for fathers. Perhaps it's because we have fewer godly fathers who have won their children's admiration. Have you noticed that fathers are depicted as idiots in movies, television, and even in cartoons? In the sitcom *Everybody Loves Raymond*, the character Debra degrades her husband by calling him an idiot whenever he makes a bad judgment. No doubt her action has influenced female viewers to use name-calling when displeased with their spouse.

A person with godly fear would never act in such a way. That person would heed God's command, "Do not seek revenge or bear a grudge against one of your people, but love your neighbor as yourself. I am the LORD" (Lev. 19:18). We show honor to God by displaying reverential esteem for others. Godly fear should motivate us to offer grace by extending an encouraging word instead of thrashing another with a rude comment.

Generally, those who tear down others have little respect for themselves. Their rude comments are desperate attempts to make themselves look better. Sadly, the results usually turn out opposite.

To have respect in any relationship, you have to be worthy of honor. Where there is abuse, apathy, domination, or controlling behavior, there is no respect. While we may have experienced this type of behavior in relationships where trust should have abounded, this is not the behavior of our God. The Bible tells us that people who practice these things don't know the love of God, nor do they fear Him. John writes, "Whoever does not love does not know God, because God is love" (1 John 4:8). Because God has demonstrated His love for us by sending His Son, He is more than worthy of our respect (Rom. 5:8).

That's not all. God is worthy of our honor because He is the creator of heaven and earth. He is Lord over all. He is the King of Kings. He is the beginning and the end. He is everlasting. His glory fills the whole earth. He is grace, truth, love, light, and life. He doesn't change, and He needs no help. His greatness is unsearchable. He is the judge of righteousness, the one and only Lawgiver. He knows our secrets and examines our hearts. He sees everything and knows all about us. He is full of loving-kindness. He was moved to save us from sin. He is merciful. He has incomparable power and strength. Nothing is too difficult for Him. He is everywhere. The highest heaven cannot contain Him. He names the stars. He has unlimited understanding. He doesn't want anyone to perish. He's slow to anger and abounds in love. He lives with the humble and does no wrong. No one can stop Him, nor can they flee His presence. He is ruler of all things. He alone is God. "You were shown these things so that you might know that the LORD is God; besides him there is no other" (Deut. 4:35).

Throughout our lifetime, we meet people we hold in high esteem. Perhaps a schoolteacher helped us achieve our goals, an aunt or uncle always stood by our side, or a childhood hero earned our admiration. While it's wonderful to know and honor special people who help us better our lives, our greatest privilege is to know and honor God. This is the beginning of wisdom (Ps. 111:10).

Who's Your Daddy?

In spite of this, the people in the book of Malachi didn't show any measure of godly fear toward the Lord. They cheated God by

withholding their tithes. Their worship was empty. They had a love
affair with materialism and they were indifferent to God's moral law.
Even the priests were corrupt. Sound familiar?

The cry of God's heart today is the same as it was then:

> "A son honors his father, and a servant his master. If I
> am a father, where is the honor due me? If I am a master,
> where is the respect due me?" says the LORD Almighty.
> "It is you, O priests, who show contempt for my name."
>   "But you ask, 'How have we shown contempt for
> your name?'" (Malachi 1:6)

Bottom line, God is asking, "Who's your daddy? Where is the
respect for the one who loves and takes care of you?" The people,
along with their priests, had lost their reverential fear of God. They
had blinded themselves to His love. They couldn't see how their sin
was an affront against God. They wearied Him with their disrespect.
They robbed Him and despised His name. Then they accused God
of withholding His love. God had not withheld His love from them,
but He did withhold His blessings because of their sin. Because of
this loss of blessing, the people were wallowing in their problems and
had forgotten how God had worked on their behalf in the past. Since
God was not behaving as they thought He should, they played the
"you don't love me" card.

When I withhold something from my children that they want,
they tend to play the "you don't love me" card too. I have to remind
my children just how good I've been to them and how my goodness
supports their survival. Likewise, in Malachi, God defended Himself

against the people's accusations by reminding them of His faithful acts of love toward them. Malachi wrote,

> "Look at how differently I've treated you, Jacob, from Esau: I loved Jacob and hated Esau. I reduced pretentious Esau to a molehill, turned his whole country into a ghost town."
>
> When Edom (Esau) said, "We've been knocked down, but we'll get up and start over, good as new," God-of-the-Angel-Armies said, "Just try it and see how far you get. When I knock you down, you stay down. People will take one look at you and say, 'Land of Evil!' and 'the God-cursed tribe!'
>
> "Yes, take a good look. Then you'll see how faithfully I've loved you and you'll want even more, saying, 'May GOD be even greater, beyond the borders of Israel!'"
> (Malachi 1:2–5 MSG)

It wasn't that God didn't love *them*. Rather, *they* didn't love God. His reproofs were meant to remind and reconcile them to His love. "As many as I love, I rebuke and chasten. Therefore be zealous and repent" (Rev. 3:19 NKJV). Though the people's perception of God had grown dim, He loved them and was willing to extend grace to anyone who would return to Him. He still does the same today.

Coming Home

When I was a little girl, I played from dawn to dusk all summer with neighborhood friends. Each day was a new adventure. At sunset, one by one the children answered their parents' call to come home. My dad whistled. No matter how far my journey carried me from home, my father knew the sound of his whistle would be heard, recognized, and obeyed. Responding to his call, I jumped on my bike and headed for home. As my house came into view, I saw my dad standing on the front porch waving. I didn't realize it then, but he didn't have to stand out there and wait for me. He could have continued about his business. Instead, he displayed a father's heart. Dad waited and watched until I was safely home. His smile and open arms let me know my arrival brought him joy.

One summer, after I had grown, our six-year-old son went missing. The sun was setting, and like my dad, I stepped onto the porch and called for him to come home. I heard no response. Frantically, his dad and I searched door-to-door for him. In house after house, all we found was disappointment. Panic surged through my body. With flashlights in hand, many of our neighbors joined the search. When we still hadn't found him, we phoned the police. My body went numb with fear. We were living out our worst nightmare—our son was lost.

Before the police arrived, a neighbor returned home and stopped in front of our house. As the side door of their van slid open, there stood our son. He had gone to the ballpark with the neighbors without our permission. Caught in disobedience, our son respected his dad and apologized through a sincere display of sorrow. He knew his fate was in his father's hands, and he was afraid his father was angry with him. Instead, our son found the comfort of a father's heart. With arms of love, my husband held our son tightly and rejoiced over his homecoming.

Maybe you've wandered into a distant land and long to come home. Perhaps you've lived your life in disrespect toward God, and you fear the consequences. You may feel like you're lost for good, but God knows where you are. You have not escaped His attention. The Father knows His children and calls them by name. Those who follow Him will find their way home and be welcomed with open arms. With a Father's heart, God is waiting and watching from the front porch of heaven for your return. When we "fear the LORD and depart from evil," He is always willing to receive us no matter how far we have roamed (Prov. 3:7 NKJV).

"The fear of the LORD teaches a man [and woman] wisdom, and humility comes before honor" (Prov. 15:33). This wisdom will be reflected not only in our relationship with God, but in fellowship with all others as well. Godly fear that results in respect for others could change our world. The possibilities are endless.

While the Bible commands us to fear God, it also commands us to love Him. This may seem like a contradiction, but it's our love for God that compels us toward passionate obedience and enables us to receive His blessings. To fear God is not to shrink back from Him in terror. It's to live an obedient life, showing admiration to the one who loves us so. Only then will we love and serve and revere Him as we should.

Understanding God's love in fearful times can be difficult. When circumstances are hard, it feels like anything other than love. Yet situations are not always as they appear. You and I must devote ourselves more to the revealed nature of God's love than to the reason of our natural minds. Only then will we experience His love to the full extent.

Bible Study: Know It—Stow It—Show It

No amount of human effort, money, or resources will lead a man or woman to find wisdom. There is only one Person who knows how to find it.

1. Read Job 28:1–21. According to verses 12–14, where does wisdom come from?

2. a. Wisdom is a practical understanding about how life works and how it should be lived. According to Job 12:13, who understands wisdom?

   b. Why do you suppose it's impossible to gain wisdom from any other source or method?

3. Write out these verses:
   Job 28:28

   Psalm 111:10

   Proverbs 1:7

   Proverbs 9:10

Isaiah 33:6

Micah 6:9

4. a. What do all of these verses have in common?

   b. How would you put this into your own words?

5. a. Read Job 28:24. What does God see?

   b. Why would it be important to have reverential fear for a
      God who knows all things?

6. Compare Job 28:28 with Proverbs 9:10. Why do you think
   fearing the Lord is wisdom? What good comes from it?

7. How do you think our world would look and act differently
   if spouses respected one another, if children honored their
   parents, and citizens obeyed the laws and authorities?

8. What is the difference between someone being afraid of God
   and someone having godly fear?

9. a. Read Romans 6:17–18. What have you been set free from? Put this into your own words.

   b. What keeps you from sin and makes you a slave to righteousness?

10. a. According to Romans 6:21, what benefits did you gain from sin?

   b. How does knowing the outcome of sin motivate you to revere and obey God?

11. a. According to Romans 6:22, what are the benefits of obedience?

   b. List some practical evidence of these benefits in your life.

12. Close your study in prayer. Ask the One who is wise to give you wisdom (James 1:5). Confess your need of Him, and commit to walk in obedience and freedom from sin by the power of His Holy Spirit. Praise God for His provision.

Chapter Ten

The Love of a Father

I knew that if I remarried after Porter died, the man would have to be someone special, because I came with a unique package—a three-year-old son. You might say it was a buy-one-get-one-free kind of deal. Not just anyone could be the recipient of such an exclusive package, so I began asking God to protect me from the wrong person until the right person came along. Quickly, I knew something was different about Pat. Whenever he invited me out, it was always a family affair. My son was included. Pat wanted to get to know us both. This caught my attention right away.

As you know, I married Pat. Things were good. I had a new husband, and my son had a new daddy. Still, I had concerns. Since Pat was not Mitch's biological father, I anxiously wondered if their relationship would develop like a father-and-son relationship should develop. It didn't take long for me to realize that anyone can "father" a child, but a real daddy is one who is around to wipe the nose and the other end, too. A daddy is eager to play on the living room floor after a long, hard day at work. He's the guy that gives up golf to coach Little League baseball, and the one who carries the child to bed after he's fallen asleep on the couch. A true dad also cares enough to discipline his son.

I don't recall what Mitch did, but I do remember his reaction to Pat's discipline was unlike anytime before.

"You're not my dad!" Mitch screamed with rage. "I hate you, I hate you!" he added between sobs.

I was shocked as I watched the two of them battle out their affections. I had never seen Mitch behave that way before. He was completely out of control and overwhelmed with anger, fear, and pain.

Pat fell to his knees and embraced our son. Mitch fought him. Without letting go, Pat spoke calmly, "You can hate me if you want, but I will always love you." Pat struggled to keep his arms around Mitch as he tried to pull loose. "You're my son. I will never leave you."

With every word Pat whispered into Mitch's ear as he held him tightly, Mitch's fears began to melt away. Suddenly, his body relaxed, and he returned his father's embrace. It was a defining moment for us all. In that instant, our faces still wet with tears, Mitch began to believe in his father's love, to accept his father's love, and to offer love in return. He didn't do it because Pat was his playmate or because he filled a certain role in Mitch's life. He did it because he had been loved—completely.

Later, as I reflected on the incident, I realized that Pat mirrored the character of our heavenly Father when he vowed to always love Mitch and never let him go. He was saying to our son as God says to us, "No matter what, I'm here for you." What a beautiful picture of 1 John 4:19: "We love Him because He first loved us" (NKJV).

Our heavenly Father is not some faraway God. He is near to us, and we can approach Him, regardless of our needs. Our Father wants to be involved in every detail of our lives. He wants to know and share in our joys and our pains. Mostly, God wants us to know His love and be confident that nothing can snatch us away from Him.

One of the biblical words for our Father God is *Abba*. It is best translated "Papa" or "Daddy." These expressions of endearment comfort me as I equate them to my earthly dad, but perhaps you've never had an earthly father to turn to in times of celebration or sorrow. Maybe your dad was absent and uncaring instead of loving and available to you. If so, you've discovered that not all people love sincerely, and you've been hurt. The good news is, no matter what you've done or what's been done to you, you have a heavenly Father, and you can cry out "Daddy!" anytime, anyplace, anywhere. You can start by allowing God to wrap His loving arms around you and wash away all your fears as He whispers to your heart, "I'm here for you—no matter what."

Worthy of Being Loved

God's love is true and reliable, but sometimes we don't feel worthy of being loved by God. Sometimes, because of things that happened in our past, we think the Lord could never love us. At other times, we let our affection for God grow dim when we experience unexpected troubles or sorrows. These types of experiences can also make us feel as if God has turned His back on us and withheld His love. This is the way I felt after Porter's death. I was trapped in Satan's lie that God didn't care. It wasn't long before my feelings toward God gave way to pure anger. With fear and trembling, I nervously wondered, "Has God taken His hands off the wheel of my life? Has He left me to spin helplessly out of control?"

Most days were a blur after I returned home from Porter's funeral. I couldn't focus on cleaning. I couldn't even concentrate on my son. Sadness was my only garment. I couldn't seem to toss it off or exchange it for something lighter and easier to wear. No, the heaviness of my pain and fear were more than I could bear at times. All I thought was, "God, where are You? Don't You care?" Perhaps you've felt the same way. We tend to think that once we belong to God, we are placed inside a spiritual bubble that protects us from all adversity, worry, and fear. We assume that experiencing peace and happiness shows we have a caring Father, but when we experience trials, we question His love. Yet the Bible tells us that even as children of God, we are not free from troubles. Jesus said, "I have told you these things, so that in me you may have peace. In this world you will have trouble. But take heart! I have overcome the world" (John 16:33).

No, God has not taken His hands off the wheel of my life or yours. He is aware of our circumstances and is in complete control. Still, when life suddenly turns stormy and unexpected events occur, we doubt God's love. Troubles in our lives don't mean that God doesn't care. During these times when we feel alone and betrayed, we must not give an ear to Satan's lies. Instead, we must trust that God is acting in love on our behalf even in dire circumstances. Even though our fears may lead us to believe otherwise, God, and what He allows into our lives, is always motivated by one thing: love.

Have you ever wondered what's on the heart of God? Is it world hunger, war, UFOs, or simply the mind-draining task of running the universe? While these things may be on His mind, you and I are the precious treasures that are on His heart. Before we were born, God knew all about us. He knew what we would fear, the troubles we would face, and the mistakes we would make. Yet He chose to love us anyway. "You did not choose me, but I chose you" (John 15:16). Therefore, we can experience His love without shame or fear, knowing that troubles don't mean God doesn't care. They mean He does care. Every move God makes on our behalf is based on love. God allows the hard things in life to develop genuine faith in us so that we are able to stand when the next storm comes our way.

Understanding this truth about God helped me to see that God is not against me. He is for me. When anxious times enter my life, I strengthen my faith by reciting what I know to be true: "Lord, I trust that You are with me. I know that You will never leave me nor forsake me. I am not alone. You care for me. You are my provider, and You have a special, perfect plan for me. It's a plan to bring me good, not bad. I don't have to be afraid, for You are faithful. What I'm experiencing now may not be what I want or what I had planned for my life, but I trust You, Lord." When we can say these things, we know our faith is becoming stronger than our fears.

There's No Fear in Love

It's not that we don't long to live in God's love. We just keep coming up short by giving into temptation. Where does that leave us? Afraid that God will punish us for our wrongdoings. I receive lots of e-mails from women who fear that God is either going to punish them on earth or is waiting to punish them in heaven because they fall short of His mark. These women are living in fear of God's punishment instead of living in the hope of His love. John writes, "There is no fear in love; but perfect love casts out fear, because fear involves torment. But he who fears has not been made perfect in love" (1 John 4:18 NKJV).

A woman who knows she is loved has nothing to fear. A wife doesn't fear a loving husband, nor does a child fear the love of his or her parents. Instead, each one thinks that the person showing love is good, and they consider themselves worthy of being loved. A person who knows and believes God loves her will not live in fear. If fear is present, the person doesn't understand God's love for her.

It's true that those who remain in sin definitely have something to dread—God's judgment. On the other hand, those who seek His forgiveness always find mercy. While sin separates us from fellowship with God, it doesn't separate us from His love. We always have an open invitation into God's presence by way of honest remorse.

The Goal of God's Love Is Transformation

In the story of the adulteress (John 8:1–11), we can see clearly how Christ's love is greater than sin. It must have been an unruly scene until Jesus stepped into the situation. Caught in the very act by the Pharisees, the woman's fate hung in the balance. I imagine she felt unbearable loneliness and fear as she lay naked in the streets at the mercy of those wanted to stone her to death. Sin does that. It separates us from God and causes us to experience aloneness and fear. This is a sure sign we need to search our souls and confess our sins so that we can have peace and enjoy God's sweet presence again. On the other hand, the feelings of aloneness and fear are not signs that God's love is absent. This truth becomes as clear as a blue sky on a bright sunny day when we realize that God is not at fault. Our lack of peace is a result of our sin.

For years, I held on to my mixed bag of emotions, blaming God and others for my fear and fury. I was alone, afraid, and angry, but I didn't think I felt these things by my choice. I was this way because others gave up on me. Porter hadn't fought hard enough to stay alive. And God—well, if He really cared, then why didn't He free me from the feelings that haunted me day and night?

Over time my eyes were opened to the real problem. Instead of looking at myself, my eyes were always on someone else. When I finally did take a good, long look at myself, I realized that I was a spoiled-rotten child of God who had stomped my foot, crossed my arms, and turned my back on God—but it wasn't going to bring Porter back. Nor was I allowing God to express His love toward me and heal my wounds. In that honest moment with myself, I let go of my anger and fear and reopened my heart to God.

Letting go is hard. It demands that we let go of something we value—not something like a piece of jewelry, but our fears, our pride, or perhaps a sense of justice or revenge. It's scary to let go of such things. But I wanted change—real change. I didn't want to be afraid anymore. Fear only caused me to mistrust and lash out against those who loved me. So I knelt down beside my bed and prayed. This time my prayer wasn't about what others had or hadn't done; it was about what I had done. I had sinned by doubting God's love. To see myself that way was to see myself outside of the scope of God's grace. Doubting God's provision had separated me from the only one who could help me. The writer to the Hebrews says, "Without faith it is impossible to please God, because anyone who comes to him must believe that he exists and that he rewards those who earnestly seek him" (Heb. 11:6). Broken before God, I asked for His forgiveness. I surrendered anew to His plan for my life. What was God's response? It was pure grace. I got up from my knees a new person. I was no longer afraid or angry—just filled with God's love.

The adulteress also found indescribable love when she came face-to-face with her sin. Finding herself in the horrible situation of being caught in the act of adultery must have caused her great shame and brokenness. But broken is always the right place to be when we're reaching out for Christ's love and forgiveness. All eyes were on Jesus as the Pharisees anxiously waited to see if Christ would condemn her. With rocks in hand, they awaited His response. Jesus said, "If any one of you is without sin, let him be the first to throw a stone at her" (John 8:7).

I imagine the woman, hardly believing her ears, staring deep into the Savior's eyes. First with great terror, but then suddenly she knew by His soft gaze that no matter what happened next, she could face it. What relief she must have felt when she heard the sounds of rocks dropping to the ground and the scattering of feet. Jesus asked,

> "Woman, where are they? Has no one condemned you?"
>
> "No one, sir," she said.
>
> "Then neither do I condemn you," Jesus declared. "Go now and leave your life of sin." (John 8:10–11)

Jesus gave this woman what every heart needs—love and forgiveness. Don't misunderstand. The woman was guilty, and according to the law of Moses, she should have been put to death. But Jesus, instead of condemning her, chose to save her. He chose to save us all by dying on the cross as payment for our sins. We must turn from our lifestyle of sin just as Christ commanded the woman to do. If we do this, you and I have this promise: "If we confess our sins, he is faithful and just and will forgive us our sins and purify us from all unrighteousness" (1 John 1:9).

Although God administers grace, forgiveness of sin doesn't mean absence of consequences. When our children disobey, we take away privileges and often send them to their room. But while they may want to stay in their room and sulk, their dad and I won't let them stay there for long. We lovingly bring them back into the family by playing a game or watching a movie together. Eventually their arms unfold and they warm up to our love. Although we may not reinstate their privileges at this point, we bring them back into the family where they know they are loved, accepted, and forgiven for their actions. Likewise, in the story of the adulteress, she still endured the consequences of being caught in the act. Everyone knew it. Nevertheless, she was forgiven.

"The goal of God's love is not to approve of our sin. It is to transform our lives through faith in His Son."[1] While we must suffer the cost of our actions, God is not out to condemn us. He's out to set us free from the chains of sin that bind us. Therefore, we have nothing to fear.

Even though Jesus was saddened by the adulteress's sin, He saw her potential. That's how He sees you and me. No matter how far we miss the mark in living out His plan for our lives, God is never ashamed to offer us His love. He's not waiting for us to mess up so that He can punish us. He's waiting to restore us. Therefore, we should never be frightened to stand in His presence before His throne of grace and mercy. It's there that we find peace and new beginnings. Our testimony becomes something like this: "You are forgiving and good, O Lord, abounding in love to all who call to you" (Ps. 86:5).

Searching for Love in All the Wrong Places

Everything we need is found in the love of God. We have no need to look elsewhere. Deep inside every person is a longing for approval and

love. God intended for His children to be blessed with His unconditional love. We see this played out in the Old Testament. Fathers
gave verbal blessings to their sons. By offering this blessing, the father
was giving approval and worth to his child. You and I thrive when we
have the love and approval of our parents. Yet, when things don't go
as we think they should, when our parents don't give their blessing,
or God doesn't behave like we expect, we not only doubt their love,
but we doubt our worthiness. This causes us to look for love and
approval in all the wrong places. Instead of seeking our true identity
and worth from our Creator, we seek it in other beings who are fragile and flawed just like us. As Brent Curtis and John Eldredge explain
in *The Sacred Romance,*

> Identity is not something that falls on us out of the
> sky. For better or for worse, identity is bestowed. We
> are who we are in relation to others. But far more
> important, we draw our identity from our impact of
> those others—if and how we affect them. We long to
> know that we make a difference in the lives of others,
> to know that we matter, that our presence cannot be
> replaced by a pet, a possession, or even another per-
> son. The awful burden of the false self is that it must
> be constantly maintained. [2]

As you and I gather information about how others perceive us,
this knowledge becomes how we identify ourselves and measure our
worth. If we fail at school, we become a "failure." If we constantly
disappoint others, we become "untrustworthy." You and I wear these

labels like badges as if they were truth. We live in fear of not being able to change the bad or maintain the good we do. All of this is based on performance. That's why, when we fail to live up to God's standard, we assume He can't love us. And yet our behavior has nothing to do with God's love for us, nor does it identify our worth. His love is never changing. It doesn't depend on what we do or don't do. God's love is constant, steady, and unconditional. The prophet Jeremiah confirms, "The LORD appeared to us in the past, saying: 'I have loved you with an everlasting love; I have drawn you with loving-kindness'" (Jer. 31:3).

On the other hand, when we do receive and trust the blessing—ideally from our parents, but ultimately from God—we find a level of fulfillment and security that cannot be realized any other way. This is so important that even God blessed His Son verbally at His baptism: "This is my Son, whom I love; with him I am well pleased" (Matt. 3:17). Following this example, Pat and I decided to bless each of our children.

When Mitch turned thirteen years old, his dad and I used his birthday as an opportunity to bless him. Every member of the family was invited for this casual, yet very special, occasion. We grilled hamburgers in the backyard and enjoyed a family game of kickball. When it came time to open the gifts, Mitch received an added bonus with each one. He received a blessing. While sitting in a circle, each family member took turns presenting our son with gifts. Before Mitch opened each present, the gift-giver shared a story or memory about Mitch and then blessed him with words of encouragement for his future. When it came time for his dad and me to give our blessings, we put our words into a letter.

As Pat read aloud, I watched Mitch receive his blessing. I'll never forget the importance of that holy moment. The hushed sound as Pat read and the faces of those listening gave evidence that more was going on than I had anticipated. Perhaps our guests were realizing their own need to be blessed.

Pat shared about all the funny things Mitch has done to bring joy into our family. He told about some of his trials such as having his appendix removed and how God was faithful. He talked about Mitch's many accomplishments and how proud we were of him. In closing, Pat made one thing very clear. If Mitch had never hit a home run or played his drums with excellence—if he had never done any of the things mentioned in the letter—we would still be proud. We would be proud simply because he is our son whom we love and with whom we are well pleased.

A Missed Blessing

All of us have this God-given need to be blessed. However, many are unable to give or receive love because of their feelings of unworthiness. Perhaps that's you. If you received harsh words as a child, you may fear harshness from God. Or maybe you couldn't get your parents' approval, so you worry if God disapproves of you too. Sadly, when blessings are withheld, most will rebel.

Esau was Jacob's older brother, but Jacob was his mother's favorite. She concocted a plan to trick Isaac, the boys' father, into giving the blessing to Jacob, the younger brother, even though it rightfully belonged to Esau, the oldest son (Gen. 27:30–38). Jacob tricked his father by wearing one of Esau's smelly hunting garments and putting goatskin on his arms to emulate his older brother's hairy body. The aging father, who had poor eyesight, never suspected he was blessing the wrong son. "When Esau heard the words of his father, he cried with an exceedingly great and bitter cry, and said to his father, 'Bless me—me also, O my father!'" (Gen. 27:34 NKJV). It was too late. Esau had been robbed of his blessing. Then, "Esau held a grudge against Jacob because of the blessing his father had given him. He said to himself, 'The days of mourning for my father are near; then I will kill my brother Jacob'" (verse 41).

Like Esau, you and I long to be blessed, but if love and acceptance were not communicated to you as a child, and if no one recognized or uncovered your potential, the results could be devastating. Perhaps you've spent your life trying to earn your parents' blessing, or you've searched for it in other places. Maybe you've withdrawn or reacted in outbursts of anger. Underlining all of these symptoms is fear—a cold, lonely depression that anxiously wonders, "Does who I am or anything I do really matter to anyone?" Yes, my friend—it matters to God.

Whether or not you received a blessing from your parents, you can receive it from God. In turn, you can also bless others. Our words have the power to either bless or curse another: "The tongue that brings healing is a tree of life, but a deceitful tongue crushes the spirit" (Prov. 15:4). Maybe you have children of your own now, and you've never known the importance of blessing them. It's never too late to let God restore the time. "So I will restore to you the years that the swarming locust has eaten" (Joel 2:25 NKJV). You can always sit down with your children and tell them what they mean to you and how proud you are of them, regardless of their age. It will do wonders for their well-being. God commands us, "Do not withhold good from those who deserve it, when it is in your power to act" (Prov. 3:27). That's a blessing.

A Blessing Received Is a Blessing Owned

The only true place to find unconditional love and acceptance is in God. He knows our need. If we listen carefully, we can hear God blessing us throughout His Word. Let His words of affirmation and love cascade over you now:

"I have loved you with an everlasting love" (Jer. 31:3). My love for you is unending.

"We have known and believed the love that God has for us. God is love, and he who abides in love abides in God, and God in him" (1 John 4:16 NKJV). Receive My love and remain in it.

"Love never fails" (1 Cor. 13:8). Others may fail you, but I never will.

"He will rest in his love for you and rejoice over you with singing" (Zeph. 3:17, paraphrased). You are My joy and delight!

"His loving-kindness is better than life itself" (Ps. 63:3, paraphrased). Nothing in this world compares with My love.

"You did not choose me, but I chose you" (John 15:16). I chose to love you long before you were ever born, spoke one word, or did one deed.

"My love and kindness will not depart from you" (Isa. 54:10, paraphrased). My love is not conditional; it will never change.

"[He has] loved us and washed us from our sins in His own blood" (Rev. 1:5 NKJV). My love covers all your sins.

"For God so loved the world that He gave His only begotten Son, that whoever believes in Him should not perish but have everlasting life" (John 3:16 NKJV). Whenever you're in doubt, remember that I gave My Son to prove My love for you.

If you needed a blessing from God, you just received one. Let His love and acceptance sink deep inside. Allow it to wash away every fear, hurt, insecurity, and doubt you've had about His love. To do that will take real Bible faith, the kind of faith that believes God is love (1 John 4:8, 16), a faith that trusts His love when everything else says otherwise.

In God's love, we have nothing to fear. We don't dread someone who loves us and has our best interest at heart. Instead, we run to him. Sometimes, like Mitch, we need to cry out to our heavenly Father and let Him reassure us of His love. Other times, we need to crawl into our Father's lap and ask Him to love us. Gladly, He will.

Being secure in God's love means we no longer have to wonder, pretend, impress, or seek acceptance elsewhere. We are certain that God is pleased with us just as we are—flaws and all. As we live carefree in His love, we are free from worry and insecurities. We become confident children of God, full of worth and potential, able to do whatever

He's designed us to do. We maintain that confidence by remaining in God's love. We remain in His love by daily practicing His presence.

Bible Study: Know It—Stow It—Show It

1. a. Rewrite Romans 5:8 in your own words.

   b. According to this verse, how did God demonstrate His love for us?

   c. What, if anything, prevents you from accepting His unconditional love?

2. Sometimes things that happen to us as children can distort the way we see God's love. Is that true for you? If so, explain.

3. a. Describe a time when a sinful action of your own made you feel guilty and unworthy of God's love.

   b. Read Romans 8:38–39. How does this verse give you the assurance that the Father loves you completely, regardless of your actions?

4. a. Describe a time when an unexpected sorrow made you feel
      like God had turned His back on you.

   b. Compare Psalm 130:7 to Isaiah 54:10. What do these two
      verses say about God's love?

   c. How, if ever, have you experienced God's unfailing love
      during a time of sorrow?

   d. How real to you right now is God's unfailing love? Why is that?

   e. What would help you stay focused on the truth that His
      love is unfailing?

5. a. Adam and Eve feared the Lord's rejection because of their
      sin. What did they do in Genesis 3:8 because of this fear?

   b. List some ways we try to hide our sin from God.

   c. What was God's response to Adam and Eve's sin (Gen.
      3:21)? What did He do to show that He still loved them?

d. What assurance does this give you today? (If it doesn't give you assurance, talk about why not.)

6. a. In the story of the adulteress (John 8:1–11), what was Jesus trying to teach the people who wanted to stone her?

b. I wrote, "Even though Jesus was saddened by the adulteress's sin, He saw her potential. That's how He sees you and me. No matter how far we miss the mark in living out His plan for our lives, God is never ashamed to offer us His love." Give an example from your life that explains this.

7. How can receiving God's blessing improve your life?

8. Who do you know that needs a blessing that you can offer?

9. Put Psalm 25:7 into your own words and make it your prayer for today.

Chapter Eleven
Practicing His Presence

Is it really possible to live in God's constant presence, free from fear and sheltered by His love? Yes, miraculously, it is. Living carefree in God's love is not only doable—it's real. It's the kind of life that Jesus lived on earth and the life He desires for each of us. "As the Father has loved me, so have I loved you. Now remain in my love" (John 15:9).

If life is meant to be wrapped in God's love, why are so many Christians living in fear and defeat? Where is our power and victory? Where is our peace that flows like a river? The real question is, if God is who He says He is and does what He says He is going to do, then why don't our lives reflect His word?

Many Christians are powerless and full of anxieties because they do not faithfully practice fellowship with God. They stand in God's shadow but don't draw near. Perhaps they feel confused, abandoned, betrayed, or afraid of God. This is not the Lord's desire. He longs to be with us.

You and I were created by God for God. That's why we exist. We were created to have an ongoing personal relationship with God. Many things in our life—such as doubt, fear, pride, apathy, and

sin—can break our fellowship with God. Yet nothing causes our relationship to go stale quicker than neglecting it all together.

To really know God, we have to spend time with Him. Knowing
about God and knowing Him personally are two different things.
We can read the Bible and acquire knowledge about God, but that
doesn't mean we know God in an intimate way. Knowing about
someone and being involved in a relationship are two different experiences. I don't just want to know about God. I want to share my
hurts and joys with Him. I want to know what's on His heart too.
I desire to hear from Him instead of doing all the talking myself.
Mostly, I want to experience His love and grace every day.

But finding time to spend with the Lord in our hurried world
is difficult for most people. In these days of modern technology, we
rarely miss anything with e-mail, voice mail, digital video recorders,
and camera phones that text message. Even though these gadgets
keep us from missing a phone call, they can also cause us to miss the
thing that matters most in life—spending time with God.

If you're like most people, you probably don't have time in the
morning to squeeze God into your already overcrowded schedule.
When the alarm clock goes off, you hit the floor running. Therein
lies the problem. If you and I were made to fellowship with God and
we don't take the time to do so, our lives suddenly become down-
right unpleasant and filled with anxiety. It doesn't have to be that
way. Jesus urges us to "abide" in God (John 15:4 NKJV).

Ever since Adam and Eve stepped out from under God's presence, the Lord has been calling us back to abiding in Him, the secret
of fearless living. Abiding in His presence makes our joy full and our
peace supreme. Abiding in Him, we embrace our friendship with

God. "Friendship?" you ask. Yes, God wants us to be His friends. Jesus said, "I no longer call you servants, because a servant does not know his master's business. Instead, I have called you friends" (John 15:15). When you and I hang out with God, we have nothing to fear.

What does it mean to "abide"? It means to remain or to stay. Paul tells us exactly where we are to stay: "For you died, and your life is now hidden with Christ in God" (Col. 3:3). That's our position, and we are to stay in Christ. We don't just run to Christ when we're scared, like a child staying in her parents' bedroom after experiencing a nightmare. Abiding in Christ means to remain in His presence during every season and turn of life. The question is, "How do we do it?"

The Best Fifteen Minutes of My Life

Have you ever experienced God's presence at church or during prayer in such a way that you wanted to stay and not leave? I have. Many times, the Lord's presence can be so real to me that I want to stay right in the center of it. Yet I have the responsibility of three children, a husband, Angel (the dog who never lives up to her name), and a ministry to manage. In spite of this, like a child who didn't want to leave her mother, I once found myself begging, "Please, Lord, teach me to live in Your presence." He whispered back only one word, "Abide."

I thought about the word *abide* and how to accomplish it. I was certain that to remain in God's presence I must try hard to keep my thoughts on Him. To be sure I did, I decided to start my day by praying and reading a devotional. I also played praise music. I was certain that singing about God would keep my thoughts on Him. It was wonderful. I praised Him continuously, and my heart was full of joy. Whatever or whoever came to mind, I took it all straight to the throne of God and said a prayer. I even found myself asking God trivial questions like, "Where did I put my cleaning gloves?" To my surprise, I remembered where I'd left them. It was amazing! If I had a need, God was right there to provide. I must say—it was the best fifteen minutes of my life!

I'm not sure how I got distracted, but it wasn't until the end of the day when I was saying good night to the Lord that I realized I had strayed from His presence. The tragic part is, I hadn't even noticed He was gone. Somewhere in the midst of the day I had stopped abiding. Naturally, my heart was broken. I had planned to abide all day and worked hard to accomplish it. Once more, I prayed, "Oh Lord, teach me to live in Your presence." As I closed my eyes, He whispered again, "Abide."

We have many faulty methods for abiding. It takes more than a token prayer, reading a few biblical words, and singing praises to have staying power. Besides, abiding is not about doing more. Abiding is about seeking God for as long as it takes for us to connect with Him. Is it possible to live a life where we are in constant contact with God all day long? It was for Jesus. So it must be possible for us, too. Actually, it's a necessity if we are going to be successful at fearless living.

How Jesus Did It

Looking at a day in the life of Jesus, we find that His day was not much different from our days (Mark 1:21–35). He got up and went to work teaching at the local synagogue. His listeners were amazed at His ability to teach, as well as His ability to stay on task when interruptions occurred. Demons were a big distraction in His day. Yet Jesus quickly handled these disturbances by telling the demons to "Get lost!"

You and I may not face many demons during our day, but we do face distractions that try to keep us from accomplishing what we need to achieve. Like Jesus, we need to identify and get rid of the distractions that waste our time and cause unnecessary worry.

Jesus was also sensitive to moments that were divine appointments from God. Not all interruptions in Christ's day, or ours, are bad. As Jesus went about teaching, He was often interrupted by the sick, the blind, and those bound in sin. What was His reaction? He stopped teaching to heal, give sight, and set the sinner free.

I wonder, "How did Christ know the difference between a distraction and a divine appointment with God?" We must not forget that while Jesus was God, He was also man. He felt the pressure and anxieties of the crowds. He knew what it was like to have people depending on Him just as we have people who are counting on us. So how did Christ handle all that responsibility without losing it? His secret is found in Mark 1:35: "Very early in the morning, while it was still dark, Jesus got up, left the house and went off to a solitary place, where he prayed."

Jesus' time with God wasn't something He tacked on to an overcrowded schedule. It was His highest priority, the time when He discovered God's priorities for His life. It's where He learned about the Father's ways and will. It's where He cast His cares and got renewed and ready for whatever the day brought along. And He stayed as long as it took to connect with God. This is precisely where we so often miss out.

Unlike Jesus, I often attempt to live life in my own strength. I think I can keep going and giving without getting replenished. Wearied by life, I often become irritated with the people I love most. When I lean on my own understanding instead of seeking God's perspective, I become overloaded with concern. That's not how I want to live. It's not how you want to live. God offers us something better—Himself. We have to go and get all He offers at the throne room of grace every day. That's where His mercies are found. I love that it's called the throne room of grace, because grace is what we need to love and serve our families, others, and God. It's where we can go to cry out, "Lord, give me the grace to live in Your power and presence today. Take my fears and fill me with Your peace, Lord. I can't carry it all, but You can carry it for me." Amazingly, God loves to answer these kinds of prayers.

Christ's time with God was also fruitful. "I am the vine; you are the branches. If a man remains in me and I in him, he will bear much fruit; apart from me you can do nothing" (John 15:5). Think of what happens when we spend enough time in God's presence for His life to change ours. If we stay in prayer long enough, God's presence shows up, and the benefits are extraordinary. Prayer guards against temptation. It helps us to clearly see God's plan. We are filled with love, joy, peace, patience, kindness, goodness, and faithfulness (Gal. 5:22). It enables us to serve God and be His witness. Prayer refreshes and lifts our spirits by smoothing away fears and doubts. It allows us to know God and fellowship with Him. Prayer empowers us for daily living. Abiding is the only way to live carefree in the care of God. He is the source that we need to connect to every day.

Plug into Your Source

The president of Southern Seminary in Kentucky shared a story with me about the first time he pastored a church. It was a small church with lots of traditions. When Sunday arrived, the young pastor was excited about giving his first sermon. He stepped up to the pulpit to present his message, but immediately he was interrupted by an elderly woman who called out, "Turn on Jesus!" Surprised by the interruption, he thought to himself, "Maybe I don't sound spiritual enough." He deepened his voice and began again. The elderly woman called out a second time, "Turn on Jesus!" This time the shaken pastor paused and prayed for God to pour out the Holy Spirit, but the woman interrupted once more, "Turn on Jesus!" As he anxiously cleared his throat, shuffled his notes, and loosened his collar, one of the deacons approached the pulpit and whispered in the pastor's ear, explaining what the woman meant. Pointing to the picture of Jesus that hung on the wall behind the pulpit, the deacon informed the young pastor of an old tradition. Each Sunday, before the retired preacher spoke, he took the cord that hung from the picture and plugged it into the outlet, thereby turning on Jesus.

How often do we forget or fail to take the time to plug into our source? I don't think the disciples forgot their need for Christ in combating their concerns and weakness. In fact, when they first heard that Jesus was going away, their hearts were deeply saddened. The disciples had gotten used to living in the constant presence of Christ. More than anyone else, they knew that without Him they could do nothing. Christ's presence was indispensable to them. They couldn't imagine life without Him. To comfort their uneasiness, Jesus gave them a promise: "But the Helper, the Holy Spirit, whom the Father will send in My name, He will teach you all things, and bring to your remembrance all things that I said to you" (John 14:26 NKJV). Through the Holy Spirit, Christ assured them that His presence was still available, and they would experience Him in an even deeper way than before. The disciples' job hadn't changed, even though Jesus would not be with them in the flesh. They were to remain in unbroken fellowship with God through the Holy Spirit. If they chose not to do this, they would be powerless in ministry and in life.

You and I don't have to go it alone either. We too have the promise of the Holy Spirit. He's ready and available to aid us in any way if we take the time to seek His presence and power. As I travel and speak to audiences across the United States, nothing gives me greater peace and assurance than knowing I have a helper. I don't have to do anything in my own power. I simply come to the throne of grace as an empty vessel, asking God to fill me with His Spirit. At functions when I'm being introduced as the speaker, by faith I look to the heavens and say, "You're on." Christ's response always soothes my nerves and quiets my fears: "Surely I am with you always, to the very end of the age" (Matt. 28:20).

A Trusting Guide

When we practice the presence of God, the Holy Spirit not only empowers us but also becomes our personal guide. "The LORD will guide you continually, and satisfy your soul in drought, and strengthen your bones; you shall be like a watered garden, and like a spring of water, whose waters do not fail" (Isa. 58:11 NKJV).

This verse came alive for me a few years ago when my mother-in-law and I took the grandkids to a water park. While the kids enjoyed the water slides, I sat by the pool. A young girl nearby caught my attention as she swam, jumped, and played in the water. A man was sticking close by her. At first I thought he was her father, but as I watched them, I realized the little girl was blind, and the man was her guide. He used his voice to direct her at play. I also noticed something else. The little girl had total trust in her guide—so much so that she played in the water without fear. She was completely free in the care of her guide.

On the drive home, I couldn't stop thinking about the blind girl and her guide. What a beautiful picture of childlike faith resting in the care of God. In truth, I'm no different from that blind girl. I can't always see what's ahead of me, but Jesus can. If I'm willing to trust Him completely as my guide, I don't have to live in fear. I can live freely as God's little girl.

Inspired by my guide who watches over me, shows me which way to go, and counsels me day and night, I penned this poem that day:

> Today at the pool I saw with my eyes,
> A blind girl swimming to my surprise.
>
> I watched amazed as she swam so free.
> I thought, "If I were blind, that would not be me."
>
> Then I noticed a man by her side.
> He must be the blind girl's guide.
>
> The little girl had such faith and trust.
> It made me realize those things were a must.
>
> How else could she so freely swim?
> How could she jump and play without him?
>
> Suddenly, as I watched, my heart grew warm,
> In a trusting relationship this is the norm.

Jesus, I thought, He is my guide.
When I can't see ahead He is there by my side.

He leads and protects as I trust and obey.
I know without Him I would never find my way.

Thank You, Lord Jesus, for giving me eyes to see,
I am never alone because You are here with me.

Anytime, anywhere, you and I can pray for assistance. We can call to our heavenly guide for direction and peace while we wash the dishes, change a diaper, drive to work, or ride in an elevator—why not, you're already looking up! When you and I choose to begin our day at the feet of Jesus, we will be more conscious of His presence throughout the day. We'll be surprised at how often we find ourselves talking to our Friend—not just about our worries and concerns, but about our joys as well. The psalmist teaches us how to begin the day:

Give ear to my words, O LORD,
consider my sighing.
Listen to my cry for help,
my King and my God, for to you I pray.
In the morning, O LORD, you hear my voice;
in the morning I lay my requests before you and wait in
    expectation. (Ps. 5:1–3)

For a long time, I failed to meet with God mainly because I didn't believe He would really answer me. I was wrong. It wasn't that

God wasn't longing to respond to my cries; I simply didn't expect Him to answer. I love that the psalmist uses the word "expectation." He not only petitioned the Lord, but he anticipated an answer. To "expect" means to have a confident belief or strong hope that a particular event will happen. Too often our fears and doubts keep us from believing in prayer, from crying out to God and anticipating a loving response.

Author and pastor Henry T. Blackaby challenges us to watch with expectation for God's answers to prayer: "Watch to see what God does [after you pray].... Make the connection between your prayer and what happens next."[1]

Jesus said it this way: "If you remain in me and my words remain in you, ask whatever you wish, and it will be given you" (John 15:7).

When my children ask something of me, they expect an answer. Then they anticipate the fulfilling of that answer. As children of God, we should do no less. We should anticipate great things from our great God. We should so eagerly expect Him to hear our cries and respond that we are looking all around in anticipation of the answer. According to Hebrews 11:1, we see God and His provisions by believing—"Now faith is being sure of what we hope for and certain of what we do not see." Let me ask you—do you hope God will answer your needs, or do you anticipate God's generous hand at work in your life? Do you wait with expectancy, or do you doubt His provision? Granted, He may seem slow at responding, but His answers are always right on time. While it would be nice if God owned the same watch that we do, we can always count on His reply—in His timing. We'll see our Guide at work directing our lives when we can say, "I will wait and watch with expectation for my God."

Peace Rules

As we wait, we have no need to fret. We can have peace. When God is present, peace rules. Isn't peace what we all want? Peace is a state of tranquility or quiet amidst anxious thoughts and emotions. It speaks of freedom. Yes, freedom. That's what we want. When the things of life haunt us—that stack of bills, new tires for the car, anxious feelings of inadequacy—don't we long for peace? Good news—we can have that kind of peace.

Jesus told His disciples, "Peace I leave with you; my peace I give you. I do not give to you as the world gives. Do not let your hearts be troubled and do not be afraid" (John 14:27). Jesus is not talking about the kind of peace we feel when a debt is finally paid. That's relief. It's not the kind of peace we experience when we can purchase that big house we've always wanted. That's gratification. The peace Christ gives is satisfying. It's peace of mind, heart, body, and soul. It's contentment in knowing that no matter what happens, we are in the care of the Almighty, and no one can snatch us away. Paul explains, "For he himself is our peace, who has made the two one and has destroyed the barrier, the dividing wall of hostility" (Eph. 2:14).

I've never watched anyone seek peace for life as earnestly as my own daughter. Plagued with anxiety from birth, she has struggled with fear her entire life. In her younger years, the panic attacks were easier to soothe. Once she entered middle school, her fears reached an all-time high. I watched helplessly as her phobias suffocated her, keeping her from experiencing the normal life of a teenage girl. Panic struck anytime she had to give an oral speech or perform in chorus. While she loves to sing, fear robbed her of her song and gave her depression instead. Nothing quieted her mind's chatter. Anxious thoughts haunted her daily: "What if someone thinks I'm strange? What if I'm not accepted? What if I date the wrong guy or follow the wrong crowd? Will God abandon me? Why am I such a scaredy-cat? What's wrong with me?"

It was obvious that the Enemy was working overtime, spooking my daughter with his lies. My goal was to help her see and acknowledge God's truth instead of the Enemy's lies. I knew that God's will for her was peace—"For God did not give us a spirit of timidity, but a spirit of power, of love and of self-discipline" (2 Tim. 1:7). Peyton clung to God and His truth. She memorized Scripture in order to combat Satan's lies. She even slept with her Bible. She was determined to remain in the presence of peace. Peyton has also learned that to be courageous, you must first be afraid. She now reaches for courage by using her fear as a stepladder constructed by her faith in God. This is the way she battles her anxieties, because she doesn't want to miss a thing.

Today she runs track, sings solos, and is a happy teenager who has learned the value of living in God's care.

Writing down and memorizing truths that counteract the Enemy's lies are good practices when we're weighed down with fear. You may need to visit your doctor for medications that can help balance your emotions while you're learning to tell truth from lies. That's okay. Our Creator made us of body, soul, and spirit. Sometimes it takes nursing all three before peace can reign.

Peace is God's will. Peace, not fear, should rule our lives. "Let the peace that comes from Christ rule in your hearts" (Col. 3:15 NLT). Peace is not something that should come and go. No, it should govern our lives. Wherever we go, whatever we do, we will encounter circumstances that are beyond our control. As long as we try to remain in control, peace is absent. When we simply remain connected to our source, God's peace is available at every turn. Once peace is secured, the things that worried us will become small, and we'll be able to rest in God's care, free from torment.

Sadly, it's our nature to try to obtain peace through our own efforts. We may pray, ask others to pray for us, and even memorize Scripture, but our anxieties cause us to work at obtaining peace instead of resting in it. J. M. Farro states that by doing this we are putting our trust in self instead of in God:

> What does the Bible say about putting our trust in someone other than God? Proverbs 28:26 says, "He who trusts in himself is a fool." The truth is, if we are not actively seeking God's help in our times of trouble, we are probably putting our trust in our own resources and abilities. … Isaiah 2:22 NLT says, "Stop putting your trust in mere humans. They are as frail as breath. How can they be of help to anyone?" … The Word of God can be our greatest source of encouragement and comfort when we're going through hard times. … In times of doubt, God's promises can give us the hope we need to stay focused on Him and His faithfulness, instead of on our circumstances.[2]

Focusing on God's faithfulness helped my daughter overcome her fears. Farro suggests that placing our trust in God leads to "an indescribable peace." As Isaiah says, "You will keep in perfect peace all who trust in you, all whose thoughts are fixed on you!" (26:3 NLT).[3]

More of God

The greatest benefit to abiding in God's presence is gaining more of Him. In His parting words to His disciples, Jesus said, "I am the true vine, and my Father is the gardener…. I am the vine; you are the branches. If a man remains in me and I in him, he will bear much fruit; apart from me you can do nothing" (John 15:1, 5). Do you get the connection? God is the gardener who tends to the grapevine. Jesus is the vine, and you and I are the branches. As we stay connected to the vine, the sap, which is the Holy Spirit, flows from the vine to the branch with the nourishment it takes to live abundantly and fruitfully. Bruce Wilkinson explains,

> Picture a place where ancient trunk meets vigorous branch. Here is the touch point, the place where abiding begins. Here is the connection where life-giving nutrients in the sap flow through to the developing fruit. The only limitation on the amount of sap that goes to the fruit is the circumference of the branch where it meets the vine. That means that the branch with the largest, least-obstructed connection with the vine is abiding the most and will have the greatest potential for a huge crop."[4]

When we are afraid, worried, panic-stricken, or we feel weak, powerless, and spiritually dry, we are never more desperate to connect with God. Being desperate is not a bad thing. It creates in us an unquenchable thirst that only God can fulfill. The psalmist describes the feeling this way: "As the deer pants for streams of water, so my soul pants for you, O God" (Ps. 42:1). Our anxieties may keep us from being productive and enjoying peace, but God nourishes us in such a way that He fills our souls to overflowing. The greatest reward of abiding is having more of God. To have more we must spend more time in His presence.

As you and I abide in Christ, soon we will be walking in unbroken fellowship with God, and His presence and peace will be evident throughout our days. Think of waking up to His presence each morning, holding His hand throughout the day, and falling asleep in His arms at night. That's carefree living! It's living as God intended—walking by His side strong, courageous, and fearless.

Bible Study: Know It—Stow It—Show It

1. Read Luke 11:1. What did the disciples ask Jesus to do?

2. Jesus gave His disciples a particular prayer to show them how to pray. Read this prayer found in Matthew 6:5–15.

   a. According to verse 6, where are we to pray?

b. What or where is your "inner room"? How often do you meet God there?

c. The first element of this prayer is to acknowledge God's holiness (verse 9). How does doing this put our fears and problems in the right perspective?

d. Think for a minute about God's holiness. How does doing this affect your perspective about your present concerns?

e. What does it take to be able to submit to God's will instead of our own (verse 10)?

f. What keeps you from giving up your rights, doubts, and will for God?

g. Which is better, your will or God's will? Why?

3. Compare Philippians 4:19 with Matthew 6:11. What do these verses tell you about your needs?

4. Even when we don't know how or what to pray, God provides. Put Romans 8:26–27 into your own words.

5. a. Matthew 6:12 asks, "Forgive us our debts, as we also have
      forgiven our debtors." How can sin hinder our prayers?

   b. How can holding a grudge against another rob us of our
      peace and bring our prayer life to a screeching halt?

   c. According to Matthew 6:15, what are the consequences of
      not forgiving others?

   d. When we seek forgiveness and offer it to others, what hap-
      pens (James 5:15–16)?

6. In Matthew 6:13, Jesus wants us to recognize how easy it is
   to fall into temptation. List some ways you are tempted that
   could be prevented by prayer.

7. a. Read Philippians 4:6–7. How does prayer help us over-
      come worry?

b. Write about a time when prayer eased your worries.

8. According to Colossians 1:9, how does prayer increase your spiritual maturity?

If we are following the model prayer Jesus has given to us, we'll come to understand how great God is and how small our concerns are in comparison to Him.

9. a. How did this chapter challenge you to practice His presence?

b. How did God speak to your heart personally?

Do you long for more of Him? He wants more of you.

Chapter Twelve
Living with Courage

Growing up, I was a huge fan of *The Wizard of Oz*. To this day, L. Frank Baum's exciting tale of a young girl and her dog, a scarecrow, a tin man, and a cowardly lion still captivates me. In my opinion, the movie remains a classic because its message still rings true: We don't need to go looking for what we already possess.

Dorothy's three friends were not in search of riches or fame. They were in search of far greater things: a brain, a heart, and courage. To obtain these great qualities, they set out for the Emerald City to see the Great Wizard who could grant them their desires. As they journeyed down the Yellow Brick Road, it became evident to the audience that the scarecrow, tin man, and lion already possessed what they were seeking. Still, they pressed on.

It wasn't until they reached the Emerald City that they discovered the wizard was no wizard at all. Not only was his title fake, his power was fake too. At first, discouragement swept the hearts of our friends. They had traveled far in hopes of great gain but had only found disappointment. In the end, though, the wizard turned out to be helpful after all. He opened their eyes so they could see themselves as they already were. The scarecrow had a brilliant mind, the tin man was a kind and loving friend, and the lion was no dandelion at all. He was the bravest of the bunch.

What about you and me? Do we see ourselves as we really are—equipped and able to face life with wisdom, love, and courage? Our God is the supplier of these qualities. Paul promises, "And God is able to make all grace abound to you, so that in all things at all times, having all that you need, you will abound in every good work" (2 Cor. 9:8). That's provision we can count on.

Like the characters in *The Wizard of Oz,* as we travel along, we will also encounter scary witches and flying monkeys in various forms that will take real knowledge, heart, and courage to face. The good news is that we have what we need to succeed.

If I Only Had a Brain

If we are going to live courageous lives where our faith is stronger than fear, we're going to need wisdom. According to the dictionary, wisdom is the ability to make sensible decisions and judgments based on knowledge and experience. Biblical wisdom is similar. God desires for us to know His patterns, His love, and His law so we can choose the wisest way to live with assurance. Peter urges us to "grow in the grace and knowledge of our Lord and Savior Jesus Christ" (2 Peter 3:18). God doesn't want us to live by any old rule. He has given us the spirit of discernment, which is the believer's ability to judge correctly and determine God's best.

God cares about every detail of our lives. He cares about who we marry, where we go to school, and which career we choose. We don't need to wring our hands in worry over these decisions, because God is interested in our lives. He knows what's best for you and me, even if we don't. The Lord wants to guide us in every decision we make. The way God guides us into all wisdom is through His Word. Our true life is revealed through the pages of the Bible. We may not find the name of our future spouse or the career we should choose in God's Word, but it will tell us what characteristics to look for in a godly mate and how to serve God through any profession. God doesn't leave us wandering in the dark, scared and unaware. He's given us the knowledge we need to live in confidence instead of fear.

Although the scarecrow was blessed with the ability to reason, he lacked faith in his knowledge. In one scene as night was falling, the scarecrow commented with uncertainty, "I think it'll get darker before it gets lighter." What did his doubt produce? Fear. In that scene, the characters locked arms tightly and moved ahead fearfully, anticipating meeting a lion, tiger, or bear—"Oh, my!" But unlike *The Wizard of Oz* characters, we don't have to guess at what's down the road. James tells us that if we lack wisdom, we can ask God, who generously provides (James 1:5).

Solomon did that very thing. When he began his reign as king, he was deeply committed to God (1 Kings 3:3). His worship gave evidence to His devotion. At Gibeon, Solomon offered a thousand burnt offerings to the Lord. In response to that expression, God appeared to Solomon in a dream and offered to give the king anything he wanted. Aware of his inability to wisely rule as king, Solomon responded, "Therefore give to Your servant an understanding heart to judge Your people, that I may discern between good and evil" (1 Kings 3:9 NKJV). Solomon could have had anything—wealth, happiness, or long life. Instead, he asked for wisdom, because he knew that being a king came with great responsibility. In order to rule with strength, courage, and faith, Solomon knew wisdom was his greatest asset. God was so impressed with Solomon's response that He gave him not only wisdom, but also wealth, health, and a peaceful reign.

Shortly after becoming king, Solomon was presented with a situation that required his new God-given wisdom. Two prostitutes appeared before him with a dispute to settle. Both women were new mothers. However, one mother accidentally took the life of her child when she rolled over on it while sleeping. In the middle of the night, she got up and exchanged her dead baby for the other mother's infant. Now, standing before the king, each mother claimed the living child as her own.

Solomon decided the case by ordering the child to be cut into two pieces with one half given to each woman. One mother agreed with the settlement; the other objected and offered to withdraw her claim in order to save the child's life. Solomon discerned the maternal instincts of the real mother, the one who wanted to spare the child's life, and decided the case in her favor (1 Kings 3:16–28). What gave Solomon the courage to order the child to be severed when the outcome could have been tragic? Wisdom.

A Miracle from Above

God's wisdom is always available. When I sensed the Lord calling me into full-time ministry, I sought the good judgment of my godly pastor. I knew that if I misinterpreted God's call, there could be devastating effects. Not only would I miss my purpose in life, but my family would be affected, as would those on the receiving end of my ministry.

I wouldn't experience the joy, fruit, or satisfaction that comes when we are doing the Father's will for our lives. Mostly, I would be serving in fear and doubt instead of passionate confidence.

For a year, my pastor and I sought the Lord together. Wisdom revealed itself in one word: "Wait." Waiting doesn't mean to sit around passively. It means to wait on God's peace for direction as we move forward in obedience to His Word. Until we have peace, we shouldn't move in any direction. My response was clear: "I wait for you, O LORD; you will answer, O Lord my God" (Ps. 38:15).

As I waited for God to direct my path, I started teaching at church and felt His peaceful nudge to return to school. I needed to brush up on my grammar skills and learn to use the computer. Little did I know that the computer would become a daily tool in my life. Each time I took one step forward, God confirmed my direction in undeniable ways. His confirmation was the confidence that both my husband and I needed to keep moving in the right direction.

I'll never forget the day I went to register for school. Pat went with me to calm my nerves. I sat in the office, filled out the required papers, and waited for the next step. We had no idea that God was about to confirm His will in such a personal way. When the student aide returned, he informed us that my first semester of school was already paid for, and I was good to go. Puzzled by his statement, we inquired about the paid fee. "According to our records," he explained, "you paid to attend our school eighteen years ago but never attended classes." He was right. I had planned on attending the state college, but instead I met a really cute guy named Porter and married him.

I was thrilled with the news. But Pat, who is an accountant, was suspicious. He explained to the boy that it's not possible for a business office of any kind to keep such a record. "They would have either refunded the money eighteen years ago or, by now, they would have credited it as income," he argued. The student aide agreed with Pat's accounting knowledge, but while he couldn't explain why the money was still there, he did know they were going to honor it. It was nothing short of God's goodness and mercy. Only He could have seen into the future and used this situation to confirm to an accountant's heart that his wife wasn't crazy. God really was calling her to serve Him. After that, Pat's uneasiness about what was happening in our lives settled into peace. He was now confident that God was leading and would continue to provide the wisdom we needed to make right decisions along with way.

You and I don't have to be listed in *Who's Who* to know what's what. All we have to do is ask God. Our first step toward bravery is to meditate on the knowledge of God. Only through God's perspective will we know how to apply wisdom to our situation to receive the assurance we need.

If I Only Had a Heart

Wisdom is only a part of the equation. To build a faith that is stronger than our fear, we must have "heart." The tin man had a heart. When his new friends cried in distress or fear, he cried too. It didn't matter that his tears caused him to rust solid. To the tin man, showing "heart" for others was worth the cost.

What does it mean to have a heart? I've often heard coaches and music instructors advise their students or team to play with "heart." It means to be passionately involved. It means to look beyond ourselves for the good of others and to endure until the very end. Jesus expressed it this way: "love your neighbor as yourself" (Matt. 19:19). That takes courage, because Christ's definition of a neighbor goes beyond those who live next door. A neighbor is anyone we meet who has a need.

When a Pharisee asked Jesus to explain who his neighbor was, Jesus responded with a story. A man traveling from Jerusalem to Jericho was attacked by robbers. The evil men stripped him naked, beat him brutally, and left him for dead. First a priest and then a Levite passed down the road, but neither stopped to help the man. Instead, they ignored him and walked on the other side of the road. Then, a Samaritan came down the road, saw the man, and had compassion on him. He washed the man's wounds, bandaged them, and took him to a nearby hotel. He gave the innkeeper enough money to pay for the man's needs (Luke 10:25–35). After sharing this story, Jesus asked,

> "Which of these three do you think was a neighbor to the man who fell into the hands of robbers?"
>
> The expert in the law replied, "The one who had mercy on him."
>
> Jesus told him, "Go and do likewise." (10:36–37)

You see, the Good Samaritan understood what it meant to "love your neighbor as yourself." Even though he could have cowered away like the others, he knew that through the power of the Holy Spirit, he was more than equipped to respond to a man in need with heartfelt love and compassion.

According to Jesus, everyone we meet is our neighbor. Yet this poses a problem for some of us. Throughout our lives, a sense of insufficiency crops up when we're faced with difficult situations concerning people. We don't want to get involved, be bothered, or take a risk of any kind. Sometimes we are simply worried about being forward or pushy with our thoughts and convictions. But we have the power to combat those fears through the Holy Spirit. Like the many insufficient but willing saints who have gone before us—Moses, Paul, Abraham Lincoln, Billy Graham, Mother Teresa, and more—we can turn inadequacy into victory by using our heart.

On the other hand, fear, lack of heart, and feelings of inadequacy only rob our witness and our service. Suppose a neighbor walks across the yard and tells you about her sister's life-threatening illness. She is upset and scared, wondering what comes after death. You sense God speaking in your heart, urging you to explain His saving grace to the woman, but inadequacy nearly drowns Him out. Feeling unsure is a normal human reaction, and following God's command requires that we acknowledge our fear. "Lord, I don't feel capable of witnessing to my neighbor," we say. "Good!" says God. "Then trust me to do it through you."

For Carrie, those were words to live by. Carrie was excited that her youth group was going to India to serve the people there. At first, she was excited about the possibility of meeting Mother Teresa and working for the Lord. Everything was going great until the plane landed. Not only could Carrie see the poverty, but she could smell it as well. Panic struck her heart, and she decided she couldn't handle it. She wanted to go home.

After speaking with her youth pastor, who reminded Carrie that she could "do everything through him who gives me strength" (Phil. 4:13), she decided to stay. That afternoon the youth group went to a nearby hospital to minister to the patients. As soon as they entered the door, the head nurse barked out orders, "You over here. You go over there!" Carrie found herself in front of a little old Indian woman who weighed about 85 pounds and was covered in her own feces. Carrie wanted to run, but the stare of the little Indian woman paralyzed her. It was as if she was trying to communicate, "Help me!" Carrie swallowed back her fear, rolled up her sleeves, and bathed the woman. After she had finished, the little Indian woman continued to stare at Carrie as if she was trying to communicate yet another need. Carrie didn't know what to do, so she paused and prayed. To her own surprise, Carrie was moved to pick the woman up and sit with her in a nearby rocking chair. As they rocked back and forth, Carrie began to sing softly, "Jesus loves you—this I know—for the Bible tells me so." Unbeknownst to Carrie, as she sang, the little old woman passed from her arms into the loving arms of Jesus. Because Carrie was willing to be courageous, the woman went home with dignity.

Heart gives us the courage to do extraordinary things with our ordinary lives, things that we never dreamed possible. For me, it always starts with a prayer: "Lord, break my heart with the things that break Yours. Give me the wisdom to see the needs of my neighbors. Supply me with strength so I can be brave enough to accomplish your work. I know this is your plan for me to serve, love, and witness to others, so I'm trusting in You to give me the courage I need to do Your will."

If I Only Had the Nerve

We will either cower away from hard situations or charge forward with courage as Carrie did. As for the cowardly lion, he did both. Of all the Oz characters, I best identify with him. Like the lion,

I believe I could do anything *if I only had the nerve.* The trouble is that in scary situations, the only nerve I have is a nervous stomach. Yet I've faced some pretty hard circumstances in my life, and I've discovered that I'm more courageous than I ever dreamed. One of the hurdles that took real courage was my first speaking engagement.

I was asked to give a devotional to the band members of a Christian school as they prepared to compete with other high school bands at the state competition. On my way to the school that fall morning, my heart was full of joy as I thanked God for allowing me the opportunity to speak truth and encouragement into these young lives. I was eager and well prepared. Yes, all was going well until I pulled into the school's parking lot.

Suddenly, I was paralyzed by fear. With my hands frozen to the steering wheel of the car, I couldn't move. I couldn't breathe. I couldn't believe I had said yes to speak to anyone! Doubts about my ability and message flooded my mind. I was in full-blown panic mode. With my hands still glued to the wheel and tears streaming down my cheeks, I turned and looked at the passenger seat. In my mind's eye, Satan was sitting there with a boastful grin painted across his devilish face. He taunted me, "What are you doing here?" Confused by fear, I responded, "I don't have a clue what I'm doing here!" At that moment I would have rather died than speak.

I had a choice to make. I could either allow my anxiety to prevent me from speaking, or I could face the platform with courage. How does one find courage when they're trembling in fear? Sometimes it comes down to deciding what is more important—the thing we need to do or yielding to our fear. You see, courage is not absence of fear as you might think. Rather, it withstands fear. Courage means being brave in spite of fear or hard circumstances. In other words, you and I have to experience fear in order to be courageous. We must use our fear like a step that enables us to reach our faith.

We all have fears and things we don't like to do. Courage is being brave enough to move through our fears. Think about fire-fighters. They have witnessed what fire can do to human flesh, just as I observed what it did to my husband. These scenes in our minds create fear. A fireman who has seen the wrath of fire's fury or tasted it himself and still does his job does so with courage.

That day in my car when fear gripped me, I searched my thoughts only to discover that my nervousness was based on pride. "What will they think of me?" I anxiously wondered. Knowing my own limitations created doubt in my mind. Leaning on my own understanding could have caused me to back away. Instead, I decided to trust God's wisdom over my own. My heart warmed as I considered what was more important. What God wanted to say to those kids through me was what mattered most. I decided that I might not be qualified to speak to others, but God could speak through me. God never calls us to do something He has not equipped us to do. He had called me to this place. I was there by divine appointment. Sure, my heart was pounding and my knees were knocking, but I chose to be brave. I chose to speak—afraid. The result was amazing. I could sense God pouring His love through me and into the hearts of those teens.

Afterward, when I recognized what God could do with a little courage, my testimony changed. "I will not die but live, and will proclaim what the LORD has done" (Ps. 118:17). That's the incredible truth about courage. It transforms the ordinary into something extraordinary. Courage can even enable a queen to risk her life for the sake of others.

Esther was a Jewish girl adopted by her uncle, Mordecai, after the death of her parents. When Esther was grown, she found favor in the eyes of King Xerxes. The king liked Esther so well he made her his queen. Wait a minute. Persian kings don't make Jewish girls their queen unless God has a plan. He did! To protect Esther, Mordecai instructed her to keep her Jewish background a secret. If the king discovered her nationality, it could mean her life.

Just when all seemed to be going well, Mordecai heard of a new law intended to kill the Jews. Although Mordecai was grieved and afraid for his people, God encouraged him. He gave him eyes to see that Esther was in a position to change the king's actions and save the Jews. Esther had a decision to make. Would she stand up and fight to save her people or keep quiet? Mordecai convinced Esther that God placed her in the position of queen to save her people. "And who knows," he said, "but that you have come to royal position for such a time as this?" (Esther 4:14). Still, this was risky business. She would have to expose her own nationality. This could mean death for Esther, too.

Despite the terrifying risk, Esther chose to live beyond herself. She chose faith over fear and shifted her focus of concern from herself to others. Risking her life, Esther asked to see the king. She revealed her true identity and uncovered another courtier's evil plot to destroy the Jews. At the same time, she appealed to the king to save her people. As a result, the king issued a new decree that allowed the Jews to defend themselves against their enemies. Amazingly, an entire nation was saved by the brave actions of one woman.

When you feel fearful, what's at the source? Are you focused on yourself? Taking our eyes off self and placing them on others helps us to see past our fears to the needs of others. Where has God placed you right now? Are you in an ungodly workplace? Perhaps you're in a bad relationship with a spouse or friend. Maybe you're living beside unbelieving neighbors or you have to care for aging parents. Like Esther, you have a decision to make. While you may face scary risks, think of the difference you could make in someone's life or a whole community! You may be the one God uses to begin a godly legacy within your family for generations to come. Perhaps you're the one who will be remembered for bringing moral values back into the family, our government, and the school system. Whatever God is calling you to do, this is His promise: "Be strong and courageous. Do not be terrified; do not be discouraged, for the LORD your God will be with you wherever you go" (Josh. 1:9). Through you and me He can touch another, perhaps even save a life. The possibilities are endless *if you only have the nerve.*

More Than Enough

Remember that courage is being brave in spite of our fear. We may never stop being afraid of high places or speaking in public, but we can use our fear to find our faith. We find our faith by doing it afraid. Rosa Parks, best known for the day she refused to give up her seat on a segregated bus, said, "When one's mind is made up, this diminishes fear; knowing what must be done does away with fear."[1] At the end, you'll find that you're more courageous than you knew.

After a while, speaking in public didn't seem so frightening to me. Did I still get butterflies in my stomach? Yes, but the need to vomit went away. About that time, I was asked to speak at my first large church. It was a Christmas community outreach event. I had never spoken to hundreds of women at one time. While I was nervous, I was also excited. When I arrived, I met with the director and her team along with the pastor and his wife. For some reason, they told me about all the big-name speakers who had spoken at this event in years past. I graciously smiled and nodded my head as terror silently crept over my entire body. I was in over my head and scared to death.

I had just enough time to go back to my hotel room, pack my bags, and make a run for it. Instead, when I entered my room, I fell on my knees beside the bed and cried out to God. "Lord, if You don't show up, I'm doomed to fail. I have nothing to give these women!" God answered profoundly. He said, "Duh." I had forgotten that God was the true communicator. He only invited me along as the mouthpiece He would use to speak to the hearts of those women. My focus was on what I could do instead of what God could do. It's funny how fear always brings us back to faith. "I sought the LORD, and he answered me; he delivered me from all my fears" (Ps. 34:4).

That night, I spoke about what God was doing in my family's life. My husband and I had just become guardians of our thirteen-year-old nephew. Intertwining Tony's story with the Christmas story, I explained how we are all orphans until we are adopted into God's forever family. What I didn't know was that someone had sponsored a table for six girls from the local girls home to attend the event. At the end I gave an invitation, and to my surprise, several people gave their lives to Christ that night, including three girls from the home. I was humbled as I watched what God had done not just through me, but in me. Then I heard Him whisper gently in my ear, "My sweet child, I didn't need a big-name speaker to speak to this audience tonight, because I-Am-Big-Enough."

Oh, friend, God is big enough for us to place our faith in Him. He's bigger than the Enemy. He's bigger than the unknown. He's bigger than sickness and death. He's bigger than your hurt. He's bigger than the war on family, changes in the workplace, terrorism, our financial state, our social state, and moral collapse. God is big enough! If you and I dare to believe that He is, then there is nothing we can't do. John Henry Newman understands this truth:

> He has not made us for naught; He has brought us thus far, in order to bring us further, in order to bring us on to the end. He will never leave us nor forsake us; so that we may boldly say, "The Lord is my Helper; I will not fear what flesh can do unto me." We may cast all our care upon Him who careth for us. What is it to us how our future path lies, if it be but His path? What is it to us whither it leads us, so that in the end it leads to Him? What is it to us what He puts upon us, so that He enables us to undergo it with a pure conscience, a true heart, not desiring anything of this world in comparison of Him? What is it to us what terror befalls us, if He be but a hand to protect and strengthen us?[2]

Like Dorothy and her friends in Oz, we don't always see the obvious—God's provision—but it's there and available, waiting to empower us beyond our imagination. Just think what your life would look like if you chose to believe that God is bigger than all your fear?

Can you imagine a fearless life? It's one that is filled with explosive power that enables you to reach your God-given potential. It starts by untangling your fears and walking straight along faith's path as you trust God to equip you for the journey. He will. So go ahead and dare to be courageous. Live out your God-given dreams; pursue your passions and abilities; take risks and expand your horizons. This is the way faith lives—stronger than all we fear.

Bible Study: Know It—Stow It—Show It

Winston Churchill once said, "Nothing in life is so exhilarating as to be shot at without result." Living a life of faith in God is a daily battle. Yet God has called His people to live as heroes and heroines of faith. And that takes courage.

1. What is God calling you to that takes real courage?
   A new job

   A new position

   A new level of faith

   To care for a grandchild or aging parents

   To surrender a desire or dream

   Other (name it)

2. What terrifies you most about fulfilling that calling?

3. a. List the risks of following that calling.

   b. What are the benefits?

   c. How is God using this experience to move you from fear to faith?

4. a. Read Joshua 1:1–9. How did God strengthen Joshua for the task ahead of him?

   b. What were the promises God made to Joshua?

   c. What did Joshua need to do in order to be prosperous and successful?

   d. How does this passage encourage you for your task at hand?

e. According to Joshua 1:5, why should we not be terrified
   or discouraged?

5. Write down a practical example from your life when you
   rested without fear in God's presence and power in a hard
   situation.

6. a. What does God instruct us to do in Joshua 1:7–8?

   b. How can following God's Word bring you success?

   c. How can meditating on and memorizing Scripture assist
      you in scary times?

7. What would you say if God asked you to lead others as Joshua
   did? Or to become a missionary like Paul? What if He's asking
   you to take a stand like Daniel in your workplace, family, or
   community? Write your response in a prayer to Him.

God wants us to respond with courage when we tackle something beyond our ability. Remember that we can move forward in faith because we always have His promised presence leading the way through anything this world throws at us. Because we have God, we have everything we need to live by faith—not fear.

Notes

Introduction

1 Charles Allen, *Victory in the Valleys,* quoted in "Fear," *Sermon Illustrations,* http://sermonillustrations.com/a-z/f/fear.htm.

Chapter 2: The Fear Factor

1 Malcolm Smith, *Freedom from Fear* (San Antonio, TX: Malcolm Smith Ministries, 1993), 15.

2 Author unknown, "God, Adam, Eve, and Your Kids," *The Messenger* (Arlington, WA: Vol. 1, Edition 12, March 2007), 16, adapted.

Chapter 3: Fashioned for Faith—Not Fear

1 Oswald Chambers, *My Utmost for His Highest* (Uhrichsville, OH: Barbour, 1963), 12.

Chapter 4: The Pressure's On

1 John Ortberg, *When the Game Is Over, It All Goes Back in the Box* (Grand Rapids, MI: Zondervan, 2007), 91–92.

Chapter 5: Family Matters

1 Adrian Rogers, *Lessons from What Every Christian Ought to Know,* MasterWork (Nashville, TN: LifeWay, 2007), 98.

2 Lesia Oesterreich, "Understanding Children: Fears," Iowa State University Extension, http://www.extension.iastate.edu/Publications/PM1529D.pdf.

3 Matthew Henry, *Commentary on the Whole Bible, vol. 1, Genesis to Deuteronomy* (Peabody, MA: Hendrickson Publishers, 1994).

Chapter 6: Learning to Trust Again

1 Louie Giglio, *I Am Not but I Know I AM,* (Colorado Springs, CO: Multnomah, 2005), 140.

Chapter 7: What's the Worst That Could Happen?

1 Corrie ten Boom, *The Hiding Place* (New York: Random House, 1982), 116.

2 Elmer L. Towns, *A Journey through the Old Testament* (Orlando, FL: Harcourt Brace Custom Publishers, 1996), 40.

3 C. S. Lewis, *The Weight of Glory* (San Francisco: HarperOne, 2001), 173.

Chapter 8: Overcoming the Fear of the Unknown

1 David Jeremiah, *Slaying the Giants in Your Life* (Nashville, TN: Thomas Nelson, 2002), 38.

2 Anne Graham Lotz, *My Heart's Cry* (Nashville, TN: W Publishing Group, 2002), 63.

Chapter 10: The Love of a Father

1 Charles Stanley, "God's Amazing Love," *In Touch,* February 2007, 8.

2 Brent Curtis and John Eldredge, *The Sacred Romance* (Nashville, TN: Thomas Nelson, 1997), 88.

Chapter 11: Practicing His Presence

1 Henry T. Blackaby, *Experiencing God: Knowing and Doing the Will of God* (Nashville, TN: B&H Publishing Group, 2008), 117.

2 J. M Farro, "A Matter of Trust," Jesus freak Hideout, http://www.jesusfreak hideout.com/devotionals/trust.asp.

3 Ibid.

4 Bruce Wilkinson, *Secrets of The Vine* (Sisters, OR: Multnomah, 2001), 95.

Chapter 12 Living with Courage

1 Rosa Parks, *Quiet Strength* (Grand Rapids, MI: Zondervan, 2000), 17.

2 John Henry Newman, *Parochial and Plain Sermons* (Fort Collins, CO: Ignatius Press, 1997), 97.

About Proverbs 31 Ministries

If you were inspired by *An Untroubled Heart* and yearn to deepen your own personal relationship with Jesus Christ, I encourage you to connect with Proverbs 31 Ministries. Proverbs 31 Ministries exists to be a trusted friend who will take you by the hand and walk by your side, leading you one step closer to the heart of God through:

- Encouragement for Today, online daily devotions
- The *P31 Woman* monthly magazine
- Daily radio program
- Books and resources
- Dynamic speakers with life-changing messages
- Online Communities
- Gather and Grow groups

To learn more about Proverbs 31 Ministries call 877-731-4663 or visit www.Proverbs31.org.

To inquire about having **Micca Campbell** speak at your event, contact Micca at MiccaCampbell@comcast.net or visit www.MiccaCampbell.com

Proverbs 31 Ministries
616-G Matthews-Mint Hill Road · Matthews, NC 28105
www.Proverbs31.org